Guide to Using the RIBA Plan of Work 2013

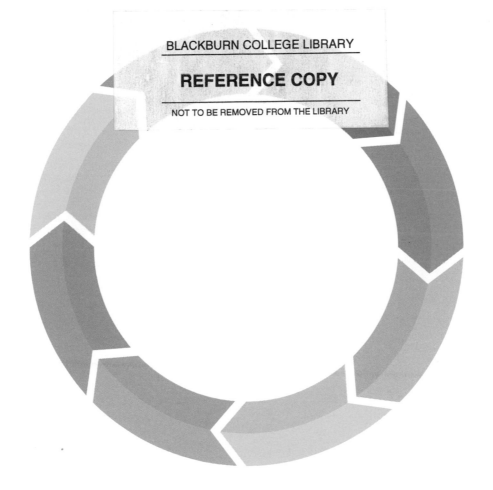

RIBA ᚛ᚉᚊ **Publishing**

www.ribaplanofwork.com

© RIBA Enterprises Ltd, 2013
Published by RIBA Publishing, 15 Bonhill Street, London EC2P 2EA

ISBN 978 1 85946 504 2

Stock code 80462

The right of Dale Sinclair to be identified as the Author of this Work has been asserted in accordance with the Copyright, Designs and Patents Act 1988 Sections 77 and 78.

British Library Cataloguing in Publication Data
A catalogue record for this book is available from the British Library.

Publisher: Steven Cross
Commissioning Editor: James Thompson
Project Editor: Alasdair Deas
Designed by Darkhorse Design and Advertising Ltd
Printed and bound by W&G Baird Ltd, Antrim

While every effort has been made to check the accuracy and quality of the information given in this publication, neither the Author nor the Publisher accepts any responsibility for the subsequent use of this information, for any errors or omissions that it may contain, or for any misunderstandings arising from it.

RIBA Publishing is part of RIBA Enterprises Ltd.
www.ribaenterprises.com

Foreword

The RIBA Plan of Work is a core RIBA document that has evolved over the years to reflect changes to the working methods of the design team. Since its inception in 1963 it has been embraced not just by architects but by the broader construction industry, where it is widely understood and used.

However, times are changing and the RIBA Plan of Work has undergone a major evolutionary change. The RIBA Plan of Work 2013 has been created in response to a number of emerging themes, including project outcomes, intelligent briefing, new handover and post-occupancy duties and Building Information Modelling (BIM).

To properly harness and use the RIBA Plan of Work 2013 it is important to understand in greater detail the many subjects that it embraces and, more importantly, how these subjects can be addressed by any project team that is adopting the Plan. This user's Guide provides that in-depth analysis.

The Guide provides a single source of information for any party contemplating the use of the RIBA Plan of Work 2013 and I would encourage all those involved in the design, construction, operation or use of a building to consider its contents. Indeed, the success of the RIBA Plan of Work 2013 will be driven by the deeper understanding of the key topics that this publication provides.

Angela Brady
President, RIBA

Contents

External reference

Frequently asked question

Chapter

1

Introduction

The RIBA Plan of Work 2013 Overview publication, available from **www.ribaplanofwork.com**, explains the rationale behind the eight project stages and eight task bars as well as explaining the logic behind the defined terms and newly introduced aspects of the RIBA Plan of Work 2013.

In addition to providing further details on these subjects, this *Guide to Using the RIBA Plan of Work 2013*:

- explains the importance of the project team and details the suite of documents required to assemble a successful project team

- underlines and considers the importance of whole life costs

- highlights the importance of Project Outcomes and why they are an essential briefing consideration

- clarifies how the RIBA Plan of Work 2013 enables the most progressive of Building Information Modelling (BIM) projects

- considers how the RIBA Plan of Work 2013 engenders best practice in health and safety, and

- demonstrates how the RIBA Plan of Work 2013 assists the implementation of sustainability measures.

It is a valuable document for any party involved in a building project during the briefing, design, construction or in-use stages, including clients, contractors and design team members. As well as providing an insight into the thinking behind the RIBA Plan of Work 2013, this guide also allows those who embrace the new RIBA Plan of Work to utilise it more effectively by understanding the reasoning behind the many issues that have been addressed during its development.

 The importance of considering and successfully assembling the project team is covered in Chapter 3 but the themes are dealt with in greater detail in the RIBA publication *Assembling a Collaborative Project Team*, which has been developed in parallel with this guide.

What is the RIBA Plan of Work?

Since its conception in 1963, the RIBA Plan of Work has been the definitive model for building design and construction processes in the UK, and has also exerted significant influence internationally. The RIBA Plan of Work framework has served both the architects' profession and the wider construction industry well.

The initial Plan of Work was conceived as a 'Plan of Work for Design Team Operations' and consisted of 12 stages and three columns that set out 'the purpose of work and decisions to be reached at each stage', 'tasks to be done' and 'the people directly involved'. This Plan of Work was updated in 1967 and again in 1973. In 1998 a major revamp was undertaken. The 12 stages were reduced to 11 by the deletion of the 'Completion' stage and, although the general thrust of each stage remained the same, only two stages retained their original titles. The 1998 RIBA Outline Plan of Work defined 'the work stages into which the process of designing building projects and administrating building contracts may be divided'. This Plan acknowledged that some variations to the work stages apply to design and build procurement, although it did not set out what these variations might be. This Plan was updated in 2007, with five stages renamed and additional descriptions of the key tasks added along with the Office of Government Commerce (OGC) Gateways, which were the old Government 'checkpoints', now renamed 'UK Government Information Exchanges'. More importantly, guidance was added on how the Plan might be adapted to different forms of procurement, although the Outline Plan of Work continued to relate to traditional procurement.

This brief synopsis of the Plan of Work's history underlines its continual evolution in response to changing trends. The RIBA Plan of Work 2013 represents the next significant evolutionary stage of the RIBA Plan of Work.

This *Guide to Using the RIBA Plan of Work 2013* sets out the reasons behind the fundamental changes, clarifies the amendments to the project stages, details changes to the key tasks to be undertaken and provides additional narrative on the core subjects that must be considered in relation to the RIBA Plan of Work 2013. More importantly, this guide sets out how the RIBA Plan of Work 2013 can be used to assemble an effective project team. This shift in emphasis from the design team to the project team is, in itself, one of the major cultural changes that the RIBA Plan of Work 2013 acknowledges and reinforces.

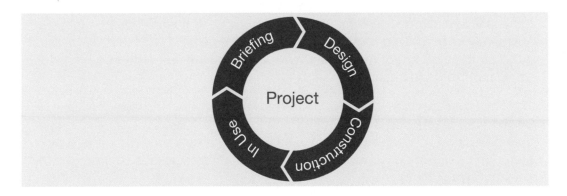

The principal purpose of the RIBA Plan of Work 2013, in line with its predecessors, is explaining to clients the circular processes involved in a building project, although these are expanded and adjusted to relate to the briefing, design, construction, maintenance, operational and in-use processes involved in a building project. Within this explanatory framework the stages continue to set particular and specific boundaries for those involved in the process. While the RIBA Plan of Work is devised by the RIBA, it is intended for use by all the parties involved in a project.

Why is a major update of the RIBA Plan of Work necessary?

The RIBA Plan of Work has continued to evolve in response to changing processes within the broader construction industry. For example, the RIBA Plan of Work 1998 acknowledged the reduced use of bills of quantities by amending Stage G to Tender Documentation and redefining the nature of Stage E. In a similar vein, the RIBA Plan of Work 2013 has been created in response to a number of drivers. The eight most important factors necessitating a major review of the RIBA Plan of Work are considered below:

1. Previous editions of the RIBA Plan of Work related to one form of procurement: traditional. The RIBA Plan of Work 2013 consultation process confirmed the fact that many different forms of procurement are used. It is now essential that the Plan of Work is relevant to any of the procurement routes currently in use.

2. Time constraints inevitably place greater pressure on front-end design work. There is a need to recalibrate the initial stages to ensure that the brief is properly developed and the project team is properly assembled.

3. The RIBA Outline Plan of Work 2007 acknowledged the potential increase in the scope of post-occupancy duties. The nature of post-occupancy duties has certainly become more onerous, but a crucial factor is the need to identify these duties at the outset of a project.

4. There has been a shift in emphasis from the design team to the project team (consisting of client + design team + contractor) and the lead designer role is frequently underplayed and misunderstood. The new RIBA Plan of Work must address the concept of the project team and redefine and reinforce the lead designer and project lead roles.

5. The RIBA Outline Plan of Work 2007 does not recognise the design work undertaken by specialist contractors. For some time now JCT contracts have acknowledged this subject by including a clause requiring such work to be stated in the Building Contract. The RIBA Plan of Work needs to embrace this common way of working.

6. The Information Age is fundamentally changing the way that we design, communicate, store and harness information. The RIBA Plan of Work has to address the implications of what some people call the 'Third Industrial Revolution'. While BIM is used as a catchall phrase for this important subject, the RIBA Plan of Work must consider the broader context.

7. Many practitioners utilise terms such as C+ or D- to refer to the point when a planning application is made. The RIBA Plan of Work must reflect these cultural 'norms' as well as acknowledging the need for pre-application activities or the increased importance of addressing any conditions attached to a planning consent.

8. The information produced at Stages D, E and F1 varies widely depending on the client, practice or project. The RIBA Plan of Work 2013 aims to provide greater clarity on this subject.

The RIBA Plan of Work is not a contractual document. Schedules of services and other contractual documents are used for contractual purposes.

What are the main changes to the RIBA Plan of Work?

On first sight, the RIBA Plan of Work 2013 appears to be a radical shift from the RIBA Outline Plan of Work 2007 (see the fold-out template at the back of this book). This is not the case. The RIBA Plan of Work 2013 maintains the tradition of explaining to clients how the briefing, design, construction, maintenance, operation and in-use processes work by mapping key activities against project stages. It still specifies the core activities undertaken at each stage. While the concept is the same, four key points need to be digested in order to understand the changes to the RIBA Plan of Work, before considering how it responds to the issues that have been highlighted:

- The RIBA Plan of Work 2013 has **eight** stages and **eight** 'task bars'. The task bars define groups of related tasks that run across all the stages. This is a shift from the 11 stages and two task bars (headed 'Description of key tasks' and 'OGC Gateways') contained in the RIBA Outline Plan of Work 2007. The new stages and task bars are set out in detail in Chapter 2.

- The RIBA Plan of Work 2013 has been developed as a template that allows a bespoke practice- or project-specific Plan of Work to be created via **www.ribaplanofwork.com**. Selecting the correct task bar from the three variable task bars for Procurement, Programme and (Town) Planning, and thus defining your own practice- or project-specific Plan, is a crucial part of the RIBA Plan of Work 2013.

- The eight stages have shifted from letters to numbers to avoid confusion in the change from eleven to eight stages and also to align with the unified work stages agreed during discussion with representatives of the broader construction industry.

- The stages relating to tendering activities have been removed from the RIBA Plan of Work 2013, as these were specific to traditional procurement; however, they have been replaced by a Procurement task bar. Procurement and tendering activities therefore continue to be an important component of the RIBA Plan of Work. Indeed, procurement activities now receive more attention as they are included at every stage.

How does the RIBA Plan of Work 2013 respond to the issues raised?

USE OF THE RIBA PLAN OF WORK 2013
In this guide, capitalised terms indicate those terms defined under each stage and in the Glossary in the RIBA Plan of Work 2013 Overview (see Chapter 10 for a list of these terms).

In response to the points raised above on the necessity for redrafting, the RIBA Plan of Work 2013:

- recommends the strategic consideration of the client's Business Case and the preparation of a Strategic Brief during the newly created Stage 0, before a more specific project brief is generated at Stage 1, along with any Feasibility Studies required to assess how the brief relates to the chosen site

- advocates the use of a specific set of documents in the creation of a project team during Stage 1 and, as part of this process, establishing communication, software, design responsibility and other protocols prior to design work commencing in earnest at Stage 2

- reflects opportunities for new post-occupancy duties during Stage 7 and, more importantly, highlights the actions required earlier in the project process to facilitate these

- acknowledges that planning applications might be submitted at Stage 2 or Stage 3 and emphasises the need to consider the risks that are created when applications are submitted at the end of Stage 2

- acknowledges the design work undertaken by specialist contractors and the need for the lead designer to integrate this work into the coordinated design during Stage 4, and

- introduces the concept of Information Exchanges to ensure that appropriate consideration is given to the information that must be exchanged during and at the end of each stage, and the need for Project Strategies to co-exist alongside the design as it develops.

New Schedules of Services for the RIBA suite of appointment documents have been produced in parallel with the RIBA Plan of Work 2013. These, along with this guide and the new RIBA publication *Assembling a Collaborative Project Team*, provide the tools necessary to successfully build a project team during Stage 1.

How does the RIBA Plan of Work 2013 differ from the 2007 Plan?

While the RIBA Plan of Work 2013 is the second major evolutionary change to the RIBA Plan of Work, it is important realise that it is not a fundamental shift from the RIBA Outline Plan of Work 2007. To emphasise this point, the transition from the 2007 stages to the 2013 stages is mapped out in the new stage definitions on pages 20 to 35, and the defined terms that have been introduced to bring greater clarity to a number of core subjects are listed in Chapter 10. The rationale behind the new task descriptions, now referred to as task bars, is set out on pages 10 to 18. This section also defines how the variable elements of the task bars can be harnessed to generate a bespoke practice- or project-specific Plan of Work.

When considering fee proposals, the areas that have the most significant impact are the integration of tendering activities within each project stage and the additional coordination work required during Stage 3.

Before considering the eight task bars and eight stages (see Chapter 2) it is important to consider that the RIBA Plan of Work 2013 represents merely the tip of the iceberg. The process outlined in Chapter 3 for assembling a successful project team is not prescriptive but it does offer the opportunity to reinvigorate the documentation necessary to support a project and the processes of briefing, designing, constructing, maintaining, operating and using a building.

 'Is it possible for the RIBA Plan of Work 2013 to be "all things to all people" and useable on small and large projects alike?'

The consultation process undertaken by the RIBA during summer 2012 suggested that traditional procurement processes are used on most smaller projects. The RIBA Plan of Work 2013 allows a practice-specific Plan of Work to be generated, based on traditional or non-traditional procurement methods but derived from the same template format, facilitating flexibility within a consistent overall framework.

Chapter

The RIBA Plan of Work 2013

How do the task bars work?

What are the eight task bars and what purpose do they serve?

What are the eight project stages?

What will a bespoke Plan of Work look like?

The RIBA Plan of Work 2013 is based on **eight** stages aligned with **eight** task bars. In this chapter we consider the purpose of each task bar, discussing how they operate in a bespoke practice- or project-specific Plan of Work. Each project stage is then examined and considered in greater detail, highlighting the specific tasks to be performed within that stage. In the extracts from the RIBA Plan of Work 2013, defined terms are set in bold type.

How do the task bars work?

In the RIBA Plan of Work 2013, eight task bars replace the 'Description of key tasks' in the RIBA Outline Plan of Work 2007. These task bars are either:

- fixed

- variable (containing options specific to a practice- or project-specific Plan of Work), or

- selectable (able to be 'switched' on or off).

The fixed bars ensure consistency across all RIBA Plan of Work 2013 documents. The ability to switch certain bars on or off and to vary the content of others provides a flexible 'kit of parts' that can be used to produce a focused and bespoke practice- or project-specific Plan of Work.

What are the eight task bars and what purpose do they serve?

Each of the eight task bars that replace the single description of key tasks in the RIBA Outline Plan of Work 2007 has a specific purpose. These are detailed below, demonstrating the degree of flexibility possible when generating a bespoke project- or practice-specific Plan of Work.

Task bar 1: **Core Objectives**

In this task bar, the Core Objectives and principal activities for each stage are set out. This task bar is fixed and is used in all versions of the RIBA Plan of Work 2013.

> **Task bars 2, 3 and 4 – the three Ps: Procurement, Programme and (Town) Planning**
>
> Procurement, programme and (town) planning activities vary widely from project to project and resolving this conundrum has been one of the biggest challenges in the creation of the RIBA Plan of Work 2013. To overcome this variability, the RIBA Plan of Work 2013 allows users to generate their own bespoke practice- or project-specific Plan of Work (a bespoke Plan can be generated using the template available at **www.ribaplanofwork.com**). During the process of generating a bespoke Plan, the user selects a specific task bar for each of these three tasks from a pull-down list and their customised Plan of Work is generated. The activities specific to each of these three variable task bars are now considered.

Task bar 2: **Procurement**

To allow for different forms of procurement, the RIBA Plan of Work 2013 has a generic procurement task bar. Users generating their bespoke Plan of Work can select the proposed procurement route from a pull-down list (see Figure 2.1 on page 12). Once the procurement route is selected, the practice- or project-specific Plan of Work that is generated will contain a task bar that includes the specific procurement and tendering activities at each stage. As a reminder, procurement activities have altered from being a stage to being a task bar.

Figure 2.1 illustrates the activities for Stages 2 to 4 that would be contained in a customised RIBA Plan of Work 2013 depending on the procurement route selected. The options available are:

- traditional contract

- one-stage design and build contract (with Contractor's Proposals defined at Stage 3)

- two-stage design and build contract (with Contractor's Proposals defined at Stage 4)

- management contract

- contractor-led contract

plus

- a 'To be determined' option where the Programme and (Town) Planning strategies are agreed but further flexibility is required in terms of procurement.

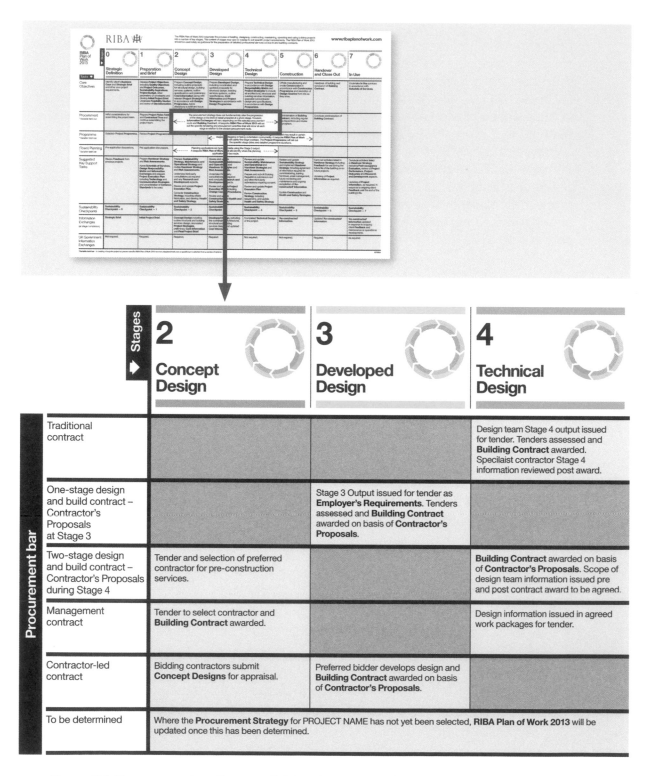

Figure 2.1 Procurement options available when generating a practice- or project-specific Plan of Work

A fundamental part of determining the procurement strategy for assembling the project team is defining the timing of contractor involvement. Further guidance on this important issue is included on page 47. The RIBA Plan of Work 2013 advocates establishing the project team during Stage 1 (refer to Chapter 3 for more detail on the most effective method of achieving a cohesive and collaborative team). A project-specific Plan of Work would typically be generated during Stage 1; however, the variable task bars have options available that allow a Plan to be generated, or finalised, during a later stage.

Where architects' practices, clients or other participants in the processes involved frequently use a specific form of procurement, such as traditional or two-stage design and build Building Contracts, they will be able to produce a practice-specific Plan of Work that can be used from the outset of each project.

Task bar 3: **Programme**

The stages of the RIBA Plan of Work 2013 are generally sequential and follow the progression of a project from commencement to completion and beyond. However, the procurement strategy, or certain client demands, may dictate that a number of stages have to occur simultaneously or overlap. The Programme task bar allows a bespoke practice- or project-specific Plan of Work to illustrate and highlight these stage overlaps. The options available are illustrated in Figure 2.2 on page 14. The option inserted into a bespoke practice- or project-specific RIBA Plan of Work 2013 is automatically selected based on the procurement route chosen. It is accepted that a multitude of further options may be possible. However, where detailed circumstances specific to a given project require an alternative approach, this should be dealt with using the Project Programme.

This task bar underlines the need on every project for a Project Programme that sets out the duration of each stage and any supporting activities. This programme should dovetail with the Design Programme(s) prepared by the lead designer, with contributions from the other designers, and the more detailed Construction Programme prepared by the contractor. A Project Programme has been a core requirement of collaborative contracts for some time, as it ensures that each party is involved in the process of agreeing timescales and is fully aware of the risks that the programme generates in relation to their specific Schedule of Services.

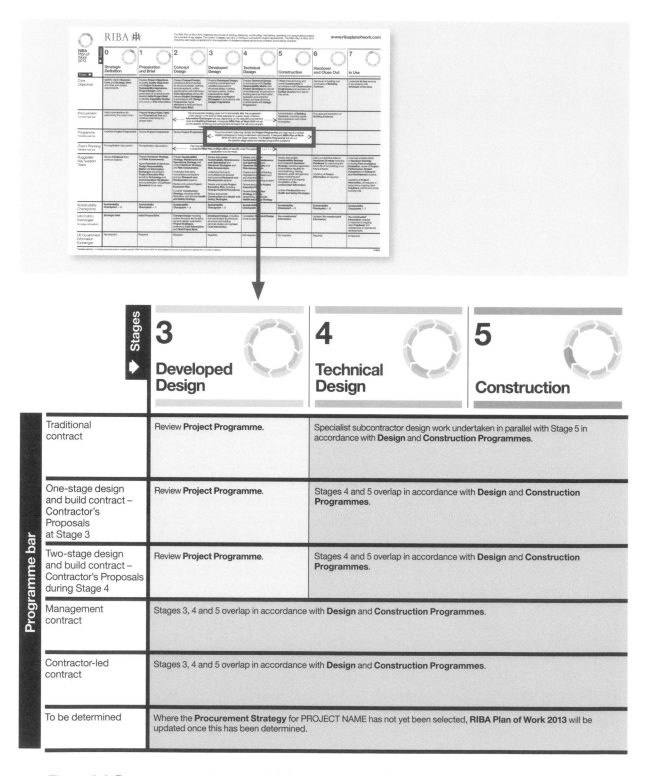

Figure 2.2 Programme options available when generating a practice- or project-specific Plan of Work

Task bar 4: **(Town) Planning**

The town planning process was identified as a key topic to be addressed by the RIBA Plan of Work 2013. Common trends identified were:

- frequent requests from clients for planning applications to be submitted earlier in the design process, typically using an enhanced Concept Design

- not all members of the design team being appointed during the initial design period

- the need to recognise the increasing amount of supporting information required for a planning application and the need for early community consultations on some projects

- the requirement, particularly on conservation projects, for very detailed design, specification and construction information to be approved before, or during, construction.

To embrace these points, the pull-down options available when generating a bespoke practice- or project-specific Plan of Work allow the user to determine whether the planning application will be made at the end of Stage 2 or Stage 3 (the recommended stage for submitting a planning application) and highlight the need to conclude planning condition submissions prior to work commencing on site. Notwithstanding the two options available for selection, it is acknowledged that in some instances the resolution of planning conditions may need to be undertaken earlier (for example, where it is a contractual imperative to do so before a client enters into a Building Contract). It is also acknowledged that on certain projects (conservation projects, for example) other planning matters may have to be concluded during Stage 5. In both scenarios, the Project Programme should be utilised to clarify these specific durations.

Where planning applications are made at the end of Stage 2, the project lead and lead designer will need to consider the level of detail to be prepared for the Stage 2 Information Exchange. On certain projects, where it is uncertain whether consent will be granted, the client may not appoint all of the designers or may appoint them on a restricted Stage 2 Schedule of Services. In these circumstances it may be necessary to include some additional activities for the project team at the start of Stage 3. A project's Risk Assessment should consider the individual project circumstances, identifying the risks created and setting out how they will be managed.

 'We are frequently commissioned to undertake only the work up to submitting a planning application. How can we make the RIBA Plan of Work 2013 relevant to our commissions?'

The RIBA Plan of Work 2013 sets out a holistic process for briefing, designing, constructing, maintaining, operating and using building projects. It is not intended to define the duties or obligations of one particular party in the process. Project-specific Schedules of Services and appointments would be required for this purpose. However, the RIBA Plan of Work 2013 does allow the specific town planning requirements of a project to be aligned to each project stage.

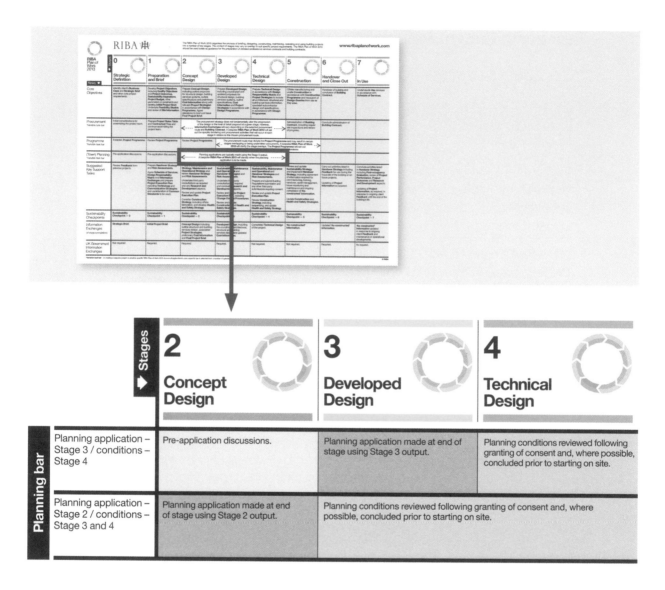

Figure 2.3 Planning process options available when generating a practice- or project-specific Plan of Work

Task bar 5: **Suggested Key Support Tasks**

The Suggested Key Support Tasks task bar:

- clarifies the activities required to achieve the Sustainability Aspirations, reducing the carbon emissions related to the building, and those required to embed Building Information Modelling (BIM) into the process

- sets out key tasks in relation to statutory requirements, such as those relating to Building Regulations submissions, project and design management protocols and roles and responsibilities

- ensures that the team is properly assembled, and that buildability, health and safety and other construction considerations and logistics are considered early in the process, by using the Project Execution Plan and Construction Strategy in the preparations.

The tasks that are listed are not mandatory; however, they do provide an appropriate level of management at each stage and assist in achieving the stated objectives.

This task bar is fixed and is used in all versions of the RIBA Plan of Work 2013.

Task bar 6: **Sustainability Checkpoints**

This task bar has been developed from the Sustainability Checkpoints included in the 2011 *Green Overlay to the RIBA Outline Plan of Work 2007*. The detailed checklists that should be completed at each checkpoint are reproduced in Chapter 8. In a bespoke practice- or project-specific Plan of Work the checklists can be highlighted by clicking on the icon next to the text.

The Sustainability Checkpoints task bar is selectable and can be switched on or off in a project- or practice-specific Plan of Work.

Task bar 7: **Information Exchanges**

This task bar provides guidance on the information that would typically be delivered at the Information Exchanges at the end of each stage. In Chapter 3 the importance of agreeing the precise extent of information and, crucially, the specific level of detail is highlighted. Preparation of the Design Responsibility Matrix and Schedule of Services are also key tasks as these impact who will produce what and when.

This topic is new to the RIBA Plan of Work and also to the RIBA appointment documents. However, given the degree of variability between practices and between projects, it is appropriate for the RIBA to provide guidance on this essential subject.

This task bar is fixed and is used in all versions of the RIBA Plan of Work 2013.

Task bar 8: **UK Government Information Exchanges**

The UK Government Information Exchanges task bar has been introduced to encourage consideration of the stages at which the UK Government requires information to be exchanged. This task bar highlights the fact that the UK Government has its own particular views on this important subject, derived from its 2011 Construction Strategy.

The UK Government recognises that, as a client, it does not need to be involved in every Information Exchange. It requires particular and specific information at each stage in order to answer the questions pertinent to a given stage. Furthermore, the UK Government is seeking data-rich information that can be used post occupancy to manage its entire estate and to allow stringent benchmarking activities to occur.

This is a developing subject and further information is best obtained from **www.bimtaskgroup.org**, including details of COBie, which will be the principal vehicle for delivering information to the UK Government as client on projects instigated in the near future.

This task bar is selectable and can be switched on or off in a bespoke project- or practice-specific Plan of Work.

What are the eight project stages?

Before considering the detail of each of the eight stages associated with the RIBA Plan of Work 2013, it is essential to bear in mind several core points:

- While the eight task bars are fixed, variable or selectable, all eight stages are fixed.

- The eight stages are referenced by numbers (0–7), rather than letters.

- The stages relating to tendering activities that have been removed from the RIBA Plan of Work 2013 have been replaced by the Procurement task bar.

- While the stages will generally occur in sequence, some may be carried out together or overlap. The Programme task bar clarifies these principles, with the Project Programme setting out the detail.

- The RIBA Plan of Work 2013 is a guidance document that allows clients to understand the key tasks that might be undertaken at each stage of a project.

- The activities listed at each stage are not intended to be contractual. Schedules of Services and other documents define the activities that are obligatory on a project.

Stage 0

Strategic Definition

Task Bar	Tasks
Core Objectives	Identify client's **Business Case** and **Strategic Brief** and other core project requirements.
Procurement Variable task bar	Initial considerations for assembling the project team.
Programme Variable task bar	Establish **Project Programme**.
(Town) Planning Variable task bar	Pre-application discussions *may be required to test the robustness of the* **Strategic Brief**.
Suggested Key Support Tasks	Review **Feedback** from previous projects.
Sustainability Checkpoints	• *Ensure that a strategic sustainability review of client needs and potential sites has been carried out, including reuse of existing facilities, building components or materials.*
Information Exchanges (at stage completion)	**Strategic Brief**.
UK Government Information Exchanges	Not required.

Stage 0 is used to ensure that the client's Business Case and the Strategic Brief have been properly considered before the Initial Project Brief is developed.

The Strategic Brief may require a review of a number of sites or alternative options, such as extensions, refurbishment or new build. By asking the right questions, the consultants, in collaboration with the client, can properly define the scope for a project, and the preparation and briefing process can then begin.

Stage 0 is a new stage in which a project is strategically appraised and defined before a detailed brief is created. This is particularly relevant in the context of sustainability, when a refurbishment or extension, or indeed a rationalised space plan, may be more appropriate than a new building. Certain activities in Stage 0 are derived from the former (RIBA Outline Plan of Work 2007) Stage A.

Stage 1

Preparation and Brief

Task Bar	Tasks
Core Objectives	Develop **Project Objectives**, including **Quality Objectives** and **Project Outcomes**, **Sustainability Aspirations**, **Project Budget**, other parameters or constraints and develop **Initial Project Brief**. Undertake **Feasibility Studies** and review of **Site Information**.
Procurement Variable task bar	Prepare **Project Roles Table** and **Contractual Tree** and continue assembling the project team.
Programme Variable task bar	Review **Project Programme**.
(Town) Planning Variable task bar	Pre-application discussions *may be required during this stage to discuss and determine the suitability of* **Feasibility Studies**.
Suggested Key Support Tasks	Prepare **Handover Strategy** and **Risk Assessments**. Agree **Schedule of Services**, **Design Responsibility Matrix** and **Information Exchanges** and prepare **Project Execution Plan** including **Technology** and **Communication Strategies** and consideration of **Common Standards** to be used. *The support tasks during this stage are focused on ensuring that the project team is properly assembled and that consideration is given to the handover of the project and the post-occupancy services that are required.*
Sustainability Checkpoints	• *Confirm that formal sustainability targets are stated in the* **Initial Project Brief**. • *Confirm that environmental requirements, building lifespan and future climate parameters are stated in the* **Initial Project Brief**. • *Have early stage consultations, surveys or monitoring been undertaken as necessary to meet sustainability criteria or assessment procedures?* • *Check that the principles of the* **Handover Strategy** *and post-completion services are included in each party's* **Schedule of Services**. • *Confirm that the Site Waste Management Plan has been implemented.*
Information Exchanges (at stage completion)	**Initial Project Brief.**
UK Government Information Exchanges	Required.

Several significant and parallel activities need to be carried out during Stage 1 Preparation and Brief to ensure that Stage 2 Concept Design is as productive as possible. These split broadly into two categories:

- developing the Initial Project Brief and any related Feasibility Studies

- assembling the project team and defining each party's roles and responsibilities and the Information Exchanges.

The preparation of the Initial Project Brief is the most important task undertaken during Stage 1. The time required to prepare it will depend on the complexity of the project.

When preparing the Initial Project Brief, it is necessary to consider:

- the project's spatial requirements

- the desired Project Outcomes, which may be derived following Feedback from earlier and similar projects

- the site or context, by undertaking site appraisals and collating Site Information, including building surveys

- the budget.

A project Risk Assessment is required to determine the risks to each party. The development of the procurement strategy, Project Programme and, in some instances, a (town) planning strategy are all part of this early risk analysis.

The importance of properly establishing the project team cannot be underestimated, given the increasing use of technology that enables remote communication and project development using BIM. For Stage 2 to commence in earnest, it is essential that the team is properly assembled. The process necessary to achieve this, and to produce the various documents required to accompany each team member's appointment, is considered in greater detail in Chapter 3.

Stage 1 merges the residual tasks from the former Stage A with the Stage B tasks that relate to carrying out preparation activities and briefing in tandem.

Stage 2

Concept Design

Task Bar	Tasks
Core Objectives	Prepare **Concept Design**, including outline proposals for structural design, building services systems, outline specifications and preliminary **Cost Information** along with relevant **Project Strategies** in accordance with **Design Programme**. Agree alterations to brief and issue **Final Project Brief**.
Procurement Variable task bar	*The Procurement activities during this stage will depend on the procurement route determined during Stage 1. The specific tasks carried out are listed under the Procurement task bar in Figure 2.1.*
Programme Variable task bar	Review **Project Programme**.
(Town) Planning Variable task bar	*The RIBA Plan of Work 2013 enables planning applications to be submitted at the end of Stage 2. However, this is not the anticipated norm, but rather an option to be exercised only in response to a specific client's needs and with due regard to the associated risks.*
Suggested Key Support Tasks	Prepare **Sustainability Strategy**, **Maintenance and Operational Strategy** and review **Handover Strategy** and **Risk Assessments**. Undertake third party consultations as required and any **Research and Development** aspects. Review and update **Project Execution Plan**. Consider **Construction Strategy**, including offsite fabrication, and develop **Health and Safety Strategy**. *During this stage a number of strategies that complement the design are prepared. These strategies consider post-occupancy and operational issues along with the consideration of buildability. Third party consultations are also essential.*
Sustainability Checkpoints	• *Confirm that formal sustainability pre-assessment and identification of key areas of design focus have been undertaken and that any deviation from the* **Sustainability Aspirations** *has been reported and agreed.* • *Has the initial Building Regulations Part L assessment been carried out?* • *Have 'plain English' descriptions of internal environmental conditions and seasonal control strategies and systems been prepared?* • *Has the environmental impact of key materials and the* **Construction Strategy** *been checked?* • *Has resilience to future changes in climate been considered?*
Information Exchanges (at stage completion)	**Concept Design** including outline structural and building services design, associated **Project Strategies**, preliminary **Cost Information** and **Final Project Brief**.
UK Government Information Exchanges	Required.

During Stage 2, the initial Concept Design is produced in line with the requirements of the Initial Project Brief.

The project team also develops, in parallel with the Concept Design, a number of Project Strategies. Their importance at this stage will depend on how they are to influence the Concept Design. For example, the Sustainability Strategy is likely to be a fundamental component of the Concept Design, whereas a security strategy may have minimal or no impact and can therefore be developed during a later stage.

It is essential to revisit the brief during this stage and it should be updated and issued as the Final Project Brief as part of the Information Exchange at the end of Stage 2.

In parallel with design activity, a number of other related tasks need to be progressed in response to the emerging design, including a review of the Cost Information, the development of a Construction Strategy, a Maintenance and Operational Strategy and a Health and Safety Strategy and updating of the Project Execution Plan.

Stage 2 maps exactly to the former Stage C.

Stage 3

Developed Design

Task Bar	Tasks
Core Objectives	Prepare **Developed Design**, including coordinated and updated proposals for structural design, building services systems, outline specifications, **Cost Information** and **Project Strategies** in accordance with **Design Programme**.
Procurement *Variable task bar*	*The Procurement activities during this stage will depend on the procurement route determined during Stage 1. The specific tasks carried out are listed under the Procurement task bar in Figure 2.1.*
Programme *Variable task bar*	*The RIBA Plan of Work 2013 enables this stage to overlap with a number of other stages depending on the selected procurement route.*
(Town) Planning *Variable task bar*	*It is recommended that planning applications are submitted at the end of this stage.*
Suggested Key Support Tasks	Review and update **Sustainability**, **Maintenance and Operational** and **Handover Strategies** and **Risk Assessments**. Undertake third party consultations as required and conclude **Research and Development** aspects. Review and update **Project Execution Plan**, including **Change Control Procedures**. Review and update **Construction** and **Health and Safety Strategies**. *During this stage it is essential to review the **Project Strategies** previously generated.*
Sustainability Checkpoints	• *Has a full formal sustainability assessment been carried out?* • *Have an interim Building Regulations Part L assessment and a design stage carbon/energy declaration been undertaken?* • *Has the design been reviewed to identify opportunities to reduce resource use and waste and the results recorded in the Site Waste Management Plan?*
Information Exchanges (at stage completion)	**Developed Design**, including the coordinated architectural, structural and building services design and updated **Cost Information**.
UK Government Information Exchanges	Required.

During this stage, the Concept Design is further developed and, crucially, the design work of the core designers is progressed until the spatial coordination exercises have been completed. This process may require a number of iterations of the design and different tools may be used, including design workshops.

By the end of Stage 3, the architectural, building services and structural engineering designs will all have been developed, and will have been checked by the lead designer, with the stage design coordinated and the Cost Information aligned to the Project Budget.

Project Strategies that were prepared during Stage 2 should be developed further and in sufficient detail to allow the client to sign them off once the lead designer has checked each strategy and verified that the Cost Information incorporates adequate allowances.

Change Control Procedures should be implemented to ensure that any changes to the Concept Design are properly considered and signed off, regardless of how they are instigated.

While specialist subcontractors will undertake their design work at Stage 4, they may provide information and guidance at Stage 3 in order to facilitate a more robust developed design.

Stage 3 maps broadly to the former Stage D and part of Stage E. The strategic difference is that in the RIBA Plan of Work 2013 the Developed Design will be coordinated and aligned with the Cost Information by the end of Stage 3. This may not increase the amount of design work required, but extra time will be needed to review information and implement any changes that arise from comments made before all the outputs are coordinated prior to the Information Exchange at the end of Stage 3.

Stage 4

Technical Design

Task Bar	Tasks
Core Objectives	Prepare **Technical Design** in accordance with **Design Responsibility Matrix** and **Project Strategies** to include all architectural, structural and building services information, specialist subcontractor design and specifications, in accordance with **Design Programme**.
Procurement *Variable task bar*	*The Procurement activities during this stage will depend on the procurement route determined during Stage 1. The specific tasks carried out are listed under the Procurement task bar in Figure 2.1.*
Programme *Variable task bar*	*The RIBA Plan of Work 2013 enables this stage to overlap with a number of other stages depending on the selected procurement route.*
(Town) Planning *Variable task bar*	*The RIBA Plan of Work 2013 suggests that any conditions attached to a planning consent are addressed during this stage, prior to work starting on site during Stage 5.*
Suggested Key Support Tasks	Review and update **Sustainability**, **Maintenance and Operational** and **Handover Strategies** and **Risk Assessments**. Prepare and submit Building Regulations submission and any other third party submissions requiring consent. Review and update **Project Execution Plan**. Review **Construction Strategy**, including sequencing, and update **Health and Safety Strategy**. *A further review of the **Project Strategies** and documentation previously generated is required during this stage.*
Sustainability Checkpoints	• *Is the formal sustainability assessment substantially complete?* • *Have details been audited for airtightness and continuity of insulation?* • *Has the Building Regulations Part L submission been made and the design stage carbon/energy declaration been updated and the future climate impact assessment prepared?* • *Has a non-technical user guide been drafted and have the format and content of the Part L log book been agreed?* • *Has all outstanding design stage sustainability assessment information been submitted?* • *Are building **Handover Strategy** and monitoring technologies specified?* • *Have the implications of changes to the specification or design been reviewed against agreed sustainability criteria?* • *Has compliance of agreed sustainability criteria for contributions by specialist subcontractors been demonstrated?*
Information Exchanges (at stage completion)	Completed **Technical Design** of the project.
UK Government Information Exchanges	Not required.

The architectural, building services and structural engineering designs are now further refined to provide technical definition of the project and the design work of specialist subcontractors is developed and concluded. The level of detail produced by each designer will depend on whether the construction on site will be built in accordance with the information produced by the design team or based on information developed by a specialist subcontractor. The Design Responsibility Matrix sets out how these key design interfaces will be managed.

Using the design coordinated during the previous stage, the designers should now be able to develop their Technical Designs independently, with a degree of autonomy. The lead designer will provide input to certain aspects, including a review of each designer's work.

Once the work of the design team has been progressed to the appropriate level of detail, as defined in the Design Responsibility Matrix and the Design Programme, specialist subcontractors and/or suppliers undertaking design work will be able to progress their design work. The lead designer and other designers, where required as part of their Schedule of Services, may have duties to review this design information and to ensure that specialist subcontractor design work is integrated with the coordinated design.

By the end of this stage, all aspects of the design will be completed, apart from minor queries arising from the site during the construction stage. In many projects, Stage 4 and 5 work occurs concurrently, particularly the specialist subcontractor design aspects.

Stage 4 comprises the residual technical work of the core design team members. At the end of Stage 4, the design work of these designers will be completed, although they may have to respond to Design Queries that arise from work undertaken on site during Stage 5. This stage also includes and recognises the importance of design work undertaken by specialist subcontractors and/ or suppliers employed by the contractor (Performance Specified Work in JCT contracts) and the need to define this work early in the process in the Design Responsibility Matrix.

Stage 5

Construction

Task Bar	Tasks
Core Objectives	Offsite manufacturing and onsite **Construction** in accordance with **Construction Programme** and resolution of **Design Queries** from site as they arise.
Procurement Variable task bar	Administration of **Building Contract**, including regular site inspections and review of progress.
Programme Variable task bar	*The RIBA Plan of Work 2013 enables this stage to overlap with a number of other stages depending on the selected procurement route.*
(Town) Planning Variable task bar	*There are no specific activities in the RIBA Plan of Work 2013, however the contractor will need to comply with any construction-specific planning conditions, such as monitoring of noise levels.*
Suggested Key Support Tasks	Review and update **Sustainability Strategy** and implement **Handover Strategy**, including agreement of information required for commissioning, training, handover, asset management, future monitoring and maintenance and ongoing compilation of **'As-constructed' Information**. Update **Construction** and **Health and Safety Strategies**. *Support tasks are now focused on health and safety on site and ensuring that the project handover and post-occupancy activities, determined earlier, are properly facilitated.*
Sustainability Checkpoints	• *Has the design stage sustainability assessment been certified?* • *Have sustainability procedures been developed with the contractor and included in the* **Construction Strategy***?* • *Has the detailed commissioning and* **Handover Strategy** *programme been reviewed?* • *Confirm that the contractor's interim testing and monitoring of construction has been reviewed and observed, particularly in relation to airtightness and continuity of insulation.* • *Is the non-technical user guide complete and the aftercare service set up?* • *Has the* **'As-constructed' Information** *been issued for post-construction sustainability certification?*
Information Exchanges (at stage completion)	**'As-constructed' Information**.
UK Government Information Exchanges	Not required.

During this stage, the building is constructed on site in accordance with the Construction Programme. Construction includes the erection of components that have been fabricated off site.

The procurement strategy and/or the designer's specific Schedule of Services will have set out the designer's duties to respond to Design Queries from site generated in relation to the design, to carry out site inspections and to produce quality reports.

The output of this stage is the 'As-constructed' Information.

Stage 5 maps to the former Stage K – Construction to Practical Completion – but also includes Stage J – Mobilisation.

Stage 6

Handover and Close Out

Task Bar	Tasks
Core Objectives	Handover of building and conclusion of **Building Contract**.
Procurement Variable task bar	Conclude administration of **Building Contract**.
Programme Variable task bar	*There are no specific activities in the RIBA Plan of Work 2013.*
(Town) Planning Variable task bar	*There are no specific activities in the RIBA Plan of Work 2013.*
Suggested Key Support Tasks	Carry out activities listed in **Handover Strategy** including **Feedback** for use during the future life of the building or on future projects. Updating of **Project Information** as required. *The priority during this stage is the successful handover of the building and concluding the **Building Contract** with support tasks focused on evaluating performance and providing **Feedback** for use on future projects. Fine tuning of the building services is likely to occur.*
Sustainability Checkpoints	• *Has assistance with the collation of post-completion information for final sustainability certification been provided?*
Information Exchanges (at stage completion)	Updated **'As-constructed' Information**.
UK Government Information Exchanges	Required.

The project team's priorities during this stage will be facilitating the successful handover of the building in line with the Project Programme and, in the period immediately following, concluding all aspects of the Building Contract, including the inspection of defects as they are rectified or the production of certification required by the Building Contract.

Other services may also be required during this period. These will be dictated by project specific Schedules of Services, which should be aligned with the procurement and Handover Strategies. Tasks in relation to the Handover Strategy can be wide-ranging and may include:

- attending Feedback workshops

- considering how any lessons learned might be applied on future projects

- undertaking tasks in relation to commissioning or ensuring the successful operation and management of the building.

Stage 6 maps broadly to the former Stage L services.

Stage 7

In use

Task Bar	Tasks
Core Objectives	Undertake **In Use** services in accordance with **Schedule of Services**.
Procurement Variable task bar	*There are no specific activities in the RIBA Plan of Work 2013.*
Programme Variable task bar	*There are no specific activities in the RIBA Plan of Work 2013.*
(Town) Planning Variable task bar	*There are no specific activities in the RIBA Plan of Work 2013.*
Suggested Key Support Tasks	Conclude activities listed in **Handover Strategy** including **Post-occupancy Evaluation**, review of **Project Performance**, **Project Outcomes** and **Research and Development** aspects. Updating of **Project Information**, as required, in response to ongoing client **Feedback** until the end of the building's life.
Sustainability Checkpoints	• *Has observation of the building operation in use and assistance with fine tuning and guidance for occupants been undertaken?* • *Has the energy/carbon performance been declared?*
Information Exchanges (at stage completion)	**'As-constructed' Information** updated in response to ongoing client **Feedback** and maintenance or operational developments.
UK Government Information Exchanges	As required.

This is a new stage within the RIBA Plan of Work. It acknowledges the potential benefits of harnessing the project design information to assist with the successful operation and use of a building.

While it is likely that many of the handover duties will be completed during Stage 6, prior to conclusion of the Building Contract, certain activities may be required or necessary afterwards. These should be confirmed in the relevant Schedule of Services.

While the end of a building's life might be considered at Stage 7, it is more likely that Stage 0 of the follow-on project or refurbishment would deal with these aspects as part of strategically defining the future of the building.

Stage 7 is a new stage.

What will a bespoke Plan of Work look like?

To provide further clarity on what a bespoke RIBA Plan of Work 2013 would contain, this publication provides two examples that have been prepared using the online tool.

Example 1 – Practice-specific Plan of Work

The first example has been prepared by Architecture Practice ABC for use on its small-scale projects. It has been prepared on the following basis:

- a traditional procurement route has been selected

- the Programme task bar will be based on this procurement route

- submission of planning application will occur at the end of Stage 3

- the Sustainability Checkpoints task bar has been switched on, and

- the UK Government Information Exchanges task bar has been switched off.

Example 2 – Project-specific Plan of Work

The second example has been prepared by Architecture Practice DEF following a workshop with the project team in relation to Project XYZ in Big City. It has been prepared on the following basis:

- the agreed procurement route, following the workshop, is two-stage design and build and this procurement option has been selected

- the Programme task bar will be based on this procurement route

- submission of planning application will occur at the end of Stage 3

- the Sustainability Checkpoints task bar has been switched off, and

- the UK Government Information Exchanges task bar has been switched on.

Further information regarding the options for the Procurement, Programme and (Town) Planning task bars is contained on pages 11 to 16. However, the best way of understanding how the tool works is to generate your own Plan of Work using the online tool at **www.ribaplanofwork.com**.

Example 1
Practice-specific Plan of Work

RIBA Plan of Work 2013

This **practice** version of the RIBA Plan of Work 2013 has been prepared by **Architecture Practice ABC** for use on its **small-scale** projects. It has been prepared on the basis of a **traditional procurement** route.

Stages	0 Strategic Definition	1 Preparation and Brief	2 Concept Design	3 Developed Design	4 Technical Design	5 Construction	6 Handover and Close Out	7 In Use
Tasks								
Core Objectives	Identify client's **Business Case** and **Strategic Brief** and other core project requirements.	Develop **Project Objectives**, including **Quality Objectives** and **Project Outcomes**, **Sustainability Aspirations**, **Project Budget**, other parameters or constraints and develop **Initial Project Brief**. Undertake **Feasibility Studies** and review of **Site Information**.	Prepare **Concept Design**, including outline proposals for structural design, building services systems, outline specifications and preliminary **Cost Information** along with relevant **Project Strategies** in accordance with **Design Programme**. Agree alterations to brief and issue **Final Project Brief**.	Prepare **Developed Design**, including coordinated and updated proposals for structural design, building services systems, outline specifications, **Cost Information** and **Project Strategies** in accordance with **Design Programme**.	Prepare **Technical Design** in accordance with **Design Responsibility Matrix** and **Project Strategies** to include all architectural, structural and building services information, specialist subcontractor design and specifications, in accordance with **Design Programme**.	Offsite manufacturing and onsite **Construction** in accordance with **Construction Programme** and resolution of **Design Queries** from site as they arise.	Handover of building and conclusion of **Building Contract**.	Undertake **In Use** services in accordance with **Schedule of Services**.
Procurement *Variable task bar	Initial considerations for assembling the project team.	Prepare **Project Roles Table** and **Contractual Tree** and continue assembling the project team.			Design team Stage 4 output issued for tender. Tenders assessed and **Building Contract** awarded. Specialist contractor Stage 4 information reviewed post award.	Administration of **Building Contract**, including regular site inspections and review of progress.	Conclude administration of **Building Contract**.	
Programme *Variable task bar	Establish **Project Programme**.	Review **Project Programme**.	Review **Project Programme**.	Review **Project Programme**.		*Stages 4 and 5 overlap*		
(Town) Planning *Variable task bar	Pre-application discussions.	Pre-application discussions.	Pre-application discussions.	Planning application made at end of stage using Stage 3 output.	Planning conditions reviewed following granting of consent and, where possible, concluded prior to starting on site.			
Suggested Key Support Tasks	Review **Feedback** from previous projects.	Prepare **Handover Strategy** and **Risk Assessments**. Agree **Schedule of Services**, **Design Responsibility Matrix** and **Information Exchanges** and prepare **Project Execution Plan** including **Technology** and **Communication Strategies** and consideration of **Common Standards** to be used.	Prepare **Sustainability Strategy**, **Maintenance and Operational Strategy** and review **Handover Strategy** and **Risk Assessments**. Undertake third party consultations as required and any **Research and Development** aspects. Review and update **Project Execution Plan**. Consider **Construction Strategy**, including offsite fabrication, and develop **Health and Safety Strategy**.	Review and update **Sustainability, Maintenance and Operational and Handover Strategies** and **Risk Assessments**. Undertake third party consultations as required and conclude **Research and Development** aspects. Review and update **Project Execution Plan**, including **Change Control Procedures**. Review and update **Construction and Health and Safety Strategies**.	Review and update **Sustainability, Maintenance and Operational and Handover Strategies** and **Risk Assessments**. Prepare and submit **Building Regulations** submission and any other third party submissions requiring consent. Review and update **Project Execution Plan**. Review **Construction Strategy**, including sequencing, and update **Health and Safety Strategy**.	Review and update **Sustainability Strategy** and implement **Handover Strategy**, including agreement of information required for commissioning, training, handover, asset management, future monitoring and maintenance and ongoing compilation of **As-constructed' Information**. Update **Construction and Health and Safety Strategies**.	Carry out activities listed in **Handover Strategy** including **Feedback** for use during the future life of the building or on future projects. Updating of **Project Information** as required.	Conclude activities listed in **Handover Strategy** including **Post-occupancy Evaluation**, review of **Project Performance, Project Outcomes and Research and Development** aspects. Updating of **Project Information**, as required, in response to ongoing client **Feedback** until the end of the building's life.
Sustainability Checkpoints	Sustainability Checkpoint – 0	Sustainability Checkpoint – 1	Sustainability Checkpoint – 2	Sustainability Checkpoint – 3	Sustainability Checkpoint – 4	Sustainability Checkpoint – 5	Sustainability Checkpoint – 6	Sustainability Checkpoint – 7
Information Exchanges (at stage completion)	**Strategic Brief**.	**Initial Project Brief**.	**Concept Design** including outline structural and building services design, associated **Project Strategies**, preliminary **Cost Information** and **Final Project Brief**.	**Developed Design**, including the coordinated architectural, structural and building services design and updated **Cost Information**.	Completed **Technical Design** of the project.	**'As-constructed' Information**.	Updated **'As-constructed' Information**.	**'As-constructed' Information** updated in response to ongoing client **Feedback** and maintenance or operational developments.
UK Government Information Exchanges								

Handwritten annotations:
- *Planning application Stage 3*
- *Review Project Programme Stage 3*
- *Traditional procurement route*
- *Sustainability Checkpoints task bar switched on*
- *UK Government Information Exchanges task bar switched off*

Variable task bar – in creating a bespoke project or practice specific RIBA Plan of Work 2013 via www.ribaplanofwork.com a specific task bar is selected from a number of options.

© RIBA

Example 2
Project-specific Plan of Work

This **project** version of the RIBA Plan of Work 2013 has been prepared by **Architecture Practice DEF** for use on its **Project XYZ**. It has been prepared on the basis of a **two-stage design and build** procurement route.

RIBA Plan of Work 2013

Tasks	0 Strategic Definition	1 Preparation and Brief	2 Concept Design	3 Developed Design	4 Technical Design	5 Construction	6 Handover and Close Out	7 In Use
Core Objectives	Identify client's **Business Case** and **Strategic Brief** and other core project requirements.	Develop **Project Objectives**, including **Quality Objectives** and **Project Outcomes**, **Sustainability Aspirations**, **Project Budget**, other parameters or constraints and develop **Initial Project Brief**. Undertake **Feasibility Studies** and review of **Site Information**.	Prepare **Concept Design**, including outline proposals for structural design, building services systems, outline specifications and preliminary **Cost Information** along with relevant **Project Strategies** in accordance with **Design Programme**. Agree alterations to brief and issue **Final Project Brief**.	Prepare **Developed Design**, including coordinated and updated proposals for structural design, building services systems, outline specifications, **Cost Information** and **Project Strategies** in accordance with **Design Programme**.	Prepare **Technical Design** in accordance with **Design Responsibility Matrix** and **Project Strategies** to include all architectural, structural and building services information, specialist subcontractor design and specifications, in accordance with **Design Programme**.	Offsite manufacturing and onsite **Construction** in accordance with **Construction Programme** and resolution of **Design Queries** from site as they arise.	Handover of building and conclusion of **Building Contract**.	Undertake **In Use** services in accordance with **Schedule of Services**.
Procurement *Variable task bar	Initial considerations for assembling the project team.	Prepare **Project Roles Table** and **Contractual Tree** and continue assembling the project team.	Tender and selection of preferred contractor for pre-construction services.		**Building Contract** awarded on basis of **Contractor's Proposals**. Scope of design team information issued pre and post contract award to be agreed.	Administration of **Building Contract**, including regular site inspections and review of progress.	Conclude administration of **Building Contract**.	
Programme *Variable task bar	Establish **Project Programme**.	Review **Project Programme**.	Review **Project Programme**.	Review **Project Programme**.	Stages 4 and 5 overlap in accordance with **Design** and **Construction Programmes**.			
(Town) Planning *Variable task bar	Pre-application discussions.	Pre-application discussions.	Pre-application discussions.	Planning application made at end of stage using Stage 3 output.	Planning conditions reviewed following granting of consent and, where possible, concluded prior to starting on site.			
Suggested Key Support Tasks	Review **Feedback** from previous projects.	Prepare **Handover Strategy** and **Risk Assessments**. Agree **Schedule of Services**, **Design Responsibility Matrix** and **Information Exchanges** and prepare **Project Execution Plan** including **Technology** and **Communication Strategies** and consideration of **Common Standards** to be used.	Prepare **Sustainability Strategy**, **Maintenance and Operational Strategy** and review **Handover Strategy** and **Risk Assessments**. Undertake third party consultations as required and any **Research and Development** aspects. Review and update **Project Execution Plan**. Consider **Construction Strategy**, including offsite fabrication, and develop **Health and Safety Strategy**.	Review and update **Sustainability, Maintenance and Operational** and **Handover Strategies** and **Risk Assessments**. Undertake third party consultations as required and conclude **Research and Development** aspects. Review and update **Project Execution Plan**, including **Change Control Procedures**. Review and update **Construction and Health and Safety Strategies**.	Review and update **Sustainability, Maintenance and Operational** and **Handover Strategies** and **Risk Assessments**. Prepare and submit **Building Regulations** submission and any other third party submissions requiring consent. Review and update **Project Execution Plan**. Review **Construction Strategy**, including sequencing, and update **Health and Safety Strategy**.	Review and update **Sustainability Strategy** and implement **Handover Strategy**, including agreement of information required for commissioning, training, handover, asset management, future monitoring and maintenance and ongoing compilation of 'As-constructed' Information. Update **Construction and Health and Safety Strategies**.	Carry out activities listed in **Handover Strategy** including **Feedback** for use during the future life of the building or on future projects. Updating of **Project Information** as required.	Conclude activities listed in **Handover Strategy** including **Post-occupancy Evaluation**, review of **Project Performance**, **Project Outcomes** and **Research and Development** aspects. Updating of **Project Information**, as required, in response to ongoing client **Feedback** until the end of the building's life.
Sustainability Checkpoints								
Information Exchanges (at stage completion)	**Strategic Brief**.	**Initial Project Brief**.	**Concept Design** including outline structural and building services design, associated **Project Strategies**, preliminary **Cost Information** and **Final Project Brief**.	**Developed Design**, including the coordinated architectural, structural and building services design and updated **Cost Information**.	Completed **Technical Design** of the project.	'As-constructed' **Information**.	Updated 'As-constructed' **Information**.	'As-constructed' **Information** updated in response to ongoing client **Feedback** and maintenance or operational developments.
UK Government Information Exchanges	Not required.	Required.	Required.	Required.	Not required.	Not required.	Required.	As required.

Handwritten annotations: "Two-stage design and build procurement route"; "Planning application Stage 3"; "Stages 4 and 5 overlap"; "Sustainability Checkpoints task bar switched off"; "UK Government Information Exchanges task bar switched on"

*Variable task bar – in creating a bespoke project or practice specific RIBA Plan of Work 2013 via www.ribaplanofwork.com a specific bar is selected from a number of options.

© RIBA

'How is a Plan of Work created if the procurement strategy is not finalised at the end of Stage 1?'

While it is recommended that a project-specific Plan of Work is created by the end of Stage 1, the pull-down options in the electronic version allow a degree of flexibility. If the procurement strategy, the (town) planning strategy or the Project Programme has not been determined by the end of Stage 1, a 'holding' bar can be placed in the project-specific Plan of Work and a new Plan generated when these items have been finalised.

 'What happens if fabrication drawings need to be reviewed as part of the tender process?'

Fabrication drawings would typically be reviewed during Stage 4. There may be a need to review proposals prepared by specialist subcontractors earlier. It is crucial to remember that the RIBA Plan of Work is a guidance document only and that it cannot possibly deal with the specific needs of every project. Detailed Schedules of Services and Project Programmes are required to address each project's precise requirements, as well as the other tools detailed in Chapter 3.

 'Will the reduction from three to two delivery stages impact on the quality of design produced?'

It is clear that the former Stage E wording has been interpreted and used in many different ways. The new Stage 3 Developed Design and Stage 4 Technical Design, aligned with the use of Information Exchanges, provide clarity, but in different ways. The Stage 3 design should be coordinated and this provides greater clarity regarding the status of the overall design. Depending on their working methods, the architect may require the production of 'exemplar' or 'key' details, which are crucial to the design at Stage 3. The core difference is that the information to be produced at Stage 3 will be strategically agreed at Stage 1, along with the fee levels.

3

Chapter

Establishing your project team

Chapter 1 highlighted the fact that the first RIBA Plan of Work published in 1963 was a 'Plan of Work for Design Team Operations'. One aspect in the evolutionary development of the RIBA Plan of Work 2013 is acknowledging the cultural shift from the design team to the project team. Before considering the subtle differences between these two teams it is important to examine why this shift has occurred:

- Clients vary: some have not interfaced with the design and construction process before; others are sophisticated, dealing with designers and contractors on a daily basis.

- More design work is undertaken by contractors' specialist subcontractors, creating greater overlap of design and construction activities.

- The trend towards greater consideration of post-occupancy aspects impacts on the design process and requires more input from clients.

The project team comprises:

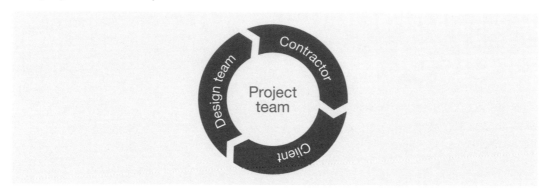

 The themes set out in this chapter are dealt with in greater depth and detail in the RIBA publication *Assembling a Collaborative Project Team*, which is designed to be complementary to this book.

How do client entities vary?

The client might be:

- an individual who is undertaking their first, and perhaps only, project

- a party with in-house design professionals, well-versed in the processes

- an organisation that outsources most aspects of the management to a design team

- an entity that undertakes all of the aspects of a project, including design, construction and operation.

This diversity of client types and the varying degree of experience that can be encountered creates complications in the early stages of a project as the type of advice and skills that a particular client requires will vary. In certain situations the client may use the services of a RIBA Client Adviser to assist them with developing the Strategic Brief or assembling the project team. Some clients may need a lot of advice regarding the design, construction and in-use stages and associated processes. Others will not require any advice and will prepare detailed tender documents, incorporating their own stringent processes, before procuring the services of the design team and the contractor. Many clients have staff or advisers who will consider the maintenance and operational aspects of a project during the design process. On certain projects, funders or other stakeholders and advisers may also be part of a client's decision-making process.

In summary, the type of client has a fundamental effect on how the project team is assembled.

How has the role of the contractor altered?

The role of the contractor has also evolved since the inception of the RIBA Plan of Work. The contractor is now frequently involved earlier in the design process and is often responsible for some or even all aspects of the design. Both of these factors have required contractors to acquire new skill sets and to develop processes that enable them to have a better understanding of the risks associated with a particular design as it develops. This changing role also requires a closer interface with the design team. The contractor's role will vary depending on the client's particular views on this subject and therefore deciding the timing for involving the contractor and determining what design aspects the contractor may be responsible for are core project decisions.

Has the role of the design team altered over the years?

The design team has not been immune to change either. A design team, particularly on larger projects, currently incorporates more individuals and parties, and many of the roles that are undertaken may be carried out by a number of parties. A greater number of specialist consultants are likely to be involved and a variety of options are available for determining who employs each member of the design team. The design team typically comprises:

- the core designers – the architect and structural and building services engineers

- the project lead and lead designer

- the cost consultant

- health and safety advisers and the building contract administrator

- additional consultants providing specialist advice

- additional consultants providing strategic advice, including client advisers.

How do these changing roles impact the RIBA Plan of Work?

The RIBA Plan of Work 2013 addresses the shift from design team to project team by setting out the tasks that need to be undertaken by the project team. It should be remembered that the RIBA Plan of Work 2013 is not a list of tasks for a particular party and that it is not intended to be a contractual document. It sets the scene for the preparation of the detailed documents that accompany professional services contracts (appointments) and the Building Contract and that will be used for the successful running and management of a project.

What tools can be used to assemble a project team?

The RIBA Plan of Work 2013 makes reference to a number of terms associated with assembling the project team – a process which should be undertaken at Stage 1 – and this chapter provides a brief overview of these. Properly assembling the project team ensures that:

- design work can be undertaken without any ambiguities in terms of responsibility

- clients can be certain that they have made sufficient allowances for fees, with the design team confident that their fee relates to the resources required to deliver the detailed Schedule of Services

- clients can proceed with confidence that the means of engaging the design team and contractor have been fully considered, and

- every party is clear about their responsibilities and the information that they will deliver at each stage.

Regardless of how the initial chemistry was created, assembling a project team requires clarification of who will do what, and when and how they will do it. Figure 3.1 illustrates how the documents referred to in the RIBA Plan of Work 2013 relate to professional services contracts and Building Contracts.

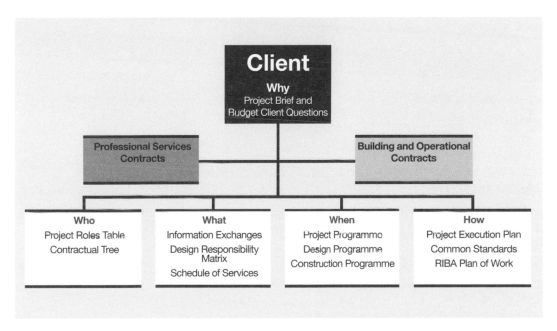

Figure 3.1 Strategic relationship between core RIBA Plan of Work 2013 documents, the client's documents and the various contracts required

The documents detailed in Figure 3.1 are referred to in the RIBA Plan of Work 2013. They have been conceived as a 'kit of parts' that allows the Who, What, When and How aspects to be considered and addressed as part of assembling the project team. More importantly, they have been compiled in a manner that allows them to be used and integrated with any professional services contracts and Building Contracts. These documents can be derived from different sources; however, *Assembling a Collaborative Project Team* considers the process for preparing them and provides a template for each document. A project manager or architectural practice may wish to use their own in-house documents or combine templates from other sources with some of the tools set out in *Assembling a Collaborative Project Team*. The important consideration is to address the subject matter before Stage 2 commences.

The composition of the project team will depend on the client's experience, their knowledge and expertise, their attitude to risk, the importance of design to a particular project, the scale and nature of the project and how much management the client intends to carry out themselves.

While the groundwork can be carried out at Stage 0, the RIBA Plan of Work 2013 strongly advocates the definition and assembling of the project team during Stage 1. This ensures that the roles and responsibilities of each organisation are clear before design work commences at Stage 2 Concept Design. The rationale is simple: if the work of each party is properly defined, design management time can be focused on the iterative design process.

The various tools set out in Figure 3.1 to deal with **who** does **what**, **when** and **how** are now considered in greater detail.

Who

A number of roles are required on every project. Core roles include:

- client

- project lead

- lead designer

- architect

- building services engineer

- civil and structural engineer

- cost consultant

- construction lead

- contract administrator

- health and safety adviser.

In addition to these core roles, specialist input may be required in relation to design or information management, masterplanning, sustainability, landscaping, planning, fire engineering, external lighting, acoustics, catering or other specialist and support roles. Even on a small project a specialist might be required; for example, an acoustician to comment on particular details adjacent to a boundary and in line with comments arising during planning discussions.

Project Roles Table

The Project Roles Table is a tool that identifies the roles required at each stage and the party responsible for each role. The process required to create the table is complicated because:

- some roles can be undertaken by a number of parties

- a commission may be restricted in its nature (i.e. up to the submission of a planning application), and

- certain roles may not be required throughout all of the project stages.

However, once the Project Roles Table is prepared, the composition of the project team should be clear, allowing detailed Schedules of Services to be prepared.

Preparation of the Project Roles Table requires consideration of when the contractor will be involved. This is an important decision as it will influence who undertakes certain roles at certain stages. To clarify this issue, the procurement options available when selecting the Procurement task bar as part of the process of producing a practice- or project-specific Plan of Work have been developed on the following basis:

- contractor involvement at the start of Stage 2 Concept Design – **contractor-led contract**

- contractor involvement at the start of Stage 3 Developed Design – **two-stage design and build contract/management contract**

- contractor involvement at the start of Stage 4 Technical Design – **one-stage design and build contract**

- contractor involvement during Stage 4 Technical Design – **traditional contract**.

On some projects the circumstances may dictate that the contractor becomes involved in the middle of a stage. The RIBA Plan of Work 2013 cannot accommodate every single situation that will arise and the specific detail in these situations should be dealt with using the Project Programme, Information Exchanges and the other tools imbedded into the Plan.

Contractual Tree

Different contractual arrangements can arise from a single Project Roles Table: for example, the lead designer appointing members of the design team rather than the client. It is for this reason that the RIBA Plan of Work 2013 advocates the preparation of a separate Contractual Tree diagram that clearly illustrates who is contracted to whom.

What

Once the allocation of roles at each stage has been agreed and the Project Roles Table prepared, together with the Contractual Tree to clarify contractual relationships, the preparation of a Design Responsibility Matrix and Schedules of Services, as well as agreement on the Information Exchanges, can progress. These are important documents as they impact on the fees of each party and ensure that the design can proceed without any ambiguities regarding who is doing what. The purpose of each of these three core tools is summarised below.

Design Responsibility Matrix

The Design Responsibility Matrix considers and allocates responsibility for each aspect of the design. A template for the matrix is included in *Assembling a Collaborative Project Team*. The matrix, and early clarity regarding design responsibilities, achieves a number of goals:

- It ensures that each designer is clear about their design responsibilities and the level of detail to be achieved for each aspect they are designing, enabling their drawings and specifications to be prepared accordingly.

- It ensures that the contractor is aware of any design responsibility obligations to be included in the Building Contract.

- It allows fees to be properly apportioned and considered by each party.

- It reduces any ambiguities about responsibilities, minimising the possibility of disputes later in the design process, when the project team is likely to be working flat out.

It is, of course, difficult to apportion precise aspects of the design before a design exists; however, the Design Responsibility Matrix allows responsibility to be defined generically at the start of the project based on experience from previous projects. The Design Responsibility Matrix can then be revisited as the design progresses and adjusted to reflect any changes in design responsibility that may be necessary.

For smaller practices that frequently work with the same structural engineer or other designers, and that perhaps use the same products and/or assemblies from project to project, the Design Responsibility Matrix can be generated and then used from one project to the next. The matrix ensures that any design responsibility being allocated to the contractor is clear from the outset, both to the client and to other members of the project team, including the contractor.

The lead designer must pay particular attention to the Design Responsibility Matrix as the matrix may affect their ability to carry out their duties and needs to dovetail with the Schedule of Services for the performance of this role.

It is important to remember that the timing of contractor involvement does not necessarily dictate the contractor's responsibilities for design: design and build forms of procurement allocate all design responsibility to the contractor whereas traditional contracts result in design responsibility remaining with the designers, although discrete elements of design responsibility may be allocated to the contractor (for example, Performance Specified Work in JCT Building Contracts).

Information Exchanges

The means of defining Information Exchanges (the information and level of detail produced at the end of each work stage) is one of the crucial topics to emerge from the development of the RIBA Plan of Work 2013. The information exchanged at the end of a stage can vary for good reason. For example, one residential client may only want a set of drawings for obtaining planning and building control approvals. Another may want detailed interior designs and full-sized joinery details. Some may require fly-through videos, models and sophisticated renderings in order to sign off the Concept Design at Stage 2. For this reason, the RIBA Plan of Work 2013 advocates that during Stage 1 the Information Exchanges at the end of each stage are agreed, along with the level of detail to be produced. The template in *Assembling a Collaborative Project Team* has been developed to assist in this process. Aligned with the Schedules of Services, a Design Programme and the Design Responsibility Matrix, it provides a comprehensive kit of parts for those undertaking the lead designer role.

What is meant by level of detail?

Although CAD information is produced 'full size', it is typically issued or exchanged as drawings in 'hard' (prints) or 'soft' (electronic) formats with the level of detail added to the CAD model dictated by the scale of the output (i.e. 1:100, 1:50, 1:5, 1:2, etc.). BIM changes this approach since such outputs are no longer required (although it is likely that 2D 'slices' through a model will continue to be used as contractual documents for some time). The level of detail question therefore progresses from an issue of scale to one of purpose. For example, if the model is being used for design discussions with a client, one level of detail is required in the model whereas a model being handed over to a specialist subcontractor (for example, to develop the curtain walling) requires a different level of detail. As this transitional subject is in an embryonic state, the Information Exchange table is conceived in a manner that considers the output scale. The transition to a digital level of detail is considered further in Chapter 6. An additional complexity is the correlation between the Design Responsibility Matrix and the Information Exchanges because the level of detail issued at Stage 4 by the core designers for work that will be undertaken by a specialist subcontractor, also during Stage 4, differs from the level of detail required to construct directly on site during Stage 5.

Schedules of Services

With the extent of design responsibility for each member of the project team covered in the Design Responsibility Matrix and the information to be produced at the end of each stage clarified in the Information Exchanges, the last component of the What aspects are Schedules of Services for all members of the project team. These schedules do not need to focus on how the members of the project team will achieve their design output; however, they are required to bring clarity on project management or design management issues. For example, the project lead may require specific management tasks to be undertaken and reporting regimes followed, and the lead designer may require other members of the design team to undertake certain duties at each stage, to be certain that coordination exercises are properly facilitated.

Schedules of Services will also be required to ensure that the services required during the briefing stages (Stages 0 and 1) are clear to each party who may be undertaking these duties. More importantly, where Project Outcomes are stated in the brief, any duties required to measure and monitor the completed project, or indeed any other project-specific post-handover duties, must be clear and included in the fee proposals of the relevant parties.

When

Programmes have historically not been an essential component of professional services contracts. The crucial cultural shift that the RIBA Plan of Work 2013 introduces is that the Project Programme and the related Design and Construction Programmes are all now important contract documents.

The Project Programme sets the strategic periods from briefing to project handover. It highlights to all parties the periods during which they have to undertake their specific duties. It may identify activities that overlap and create risk and it is therefore essential that the Project Programme is prepared and agreed prior to any appointments being made.

The lead designer may also wish to prepare a Design Programme to assist in the management of the design. This programme, and the Construction Programme prepared by the contractor, should adhere to the dates set out in the more strategic Project Programme.

How

The need for project protocols and processes will depend on the size and complexity of a project and the number of organisations involved. However, even on a small project a Project Execution Plan can be a useful document and can be used to corral contact information, the Contractual Tree (project organogram), communication protocols or other information that may be of use to the client and the project team. On larger projects, the document might be referred to as the project quality plan. Regardless of its name, the contents should be similar and might, as a minimum, contain:

- a description of the project (a summary of the brief)

- a project directory (containing contact names and details)

- the Project Roles Table

- the Contractual Tree

- the Design Responsibility Matrix

- Information Exchanges

- the Project Programme (Design and Construction Programmes might be included or referred to)

- the Communication Strategy

- company organisation charts (details of each party's team on larger projects)

- the Technology Strategy (detailing the software, and hardware, that will be used)

- CAD/BIM manual (detailing drawing numbering or other CAD/BIM protocols), and

- Change Control Procedures.

Historically, practices have utilised their own internal processes; however, BIM requires a project team to utilise Common Standards and working methods, a process that is complicated by compatibility and interoperability issues. The Technology Strategy, Communication Strategy, CAD/BIM manual and Change Control Procedures are therefore crucial components of the Project Execution Plan. These topics are considered in greater detail in Chapter 6.

 Depending on circumstances, the Project Execution Plan may be contractual or non-contractual. It may also make reference to a number of British Standards and other industry standards. These standards are considered further in *Assembling a Collaborative Project Team*.

Conclusion

The documents detailed in this chapter have been considered in a manner that allows the best possible project team to be created in line with a client's particular objectives. The documents can be applied regardless of project size and can accompany professional services contracts and Building Contracts.

The project team can then progress to Stage 2 confident in the knowledge that many of the issues that typically arise and cause problems on a project have already been addressed.

Chapter

Defining whole
life costs

What are whole life costs and why are they crucial?

How does the RIBA Plan of Work 2013 assist consideration of whole life costs?

What is the relationship between whole life costs and Project Outcomes?

The RIBA Plan of Work 2013 places greater emphasis on what happens post handover, when a building is 'in use', than previous versions of the Plan of Work. This includes considering the services that facilitate a successful handover and services which assist with the fine tuning of operational aspects until a building is performing as anticipated.

It takes into account whole life costs, including the running costs of the building, and also extends to consideration of 'softer' issues, such as the impact of the building on its occupants, users and surroundings. All of these matters can be seen as the Project Outcomes.

Importantly, the RIBA Plan of Work 2013 considers the tasks that must be undertaken in earlier stages in order to facilitate these outcomes. They are integral to the design process and have a significant bearing on a project's long-term success.

Whole life costs are considered in this chapter while Project Outcomes are dealt with in Chapter 5 and the importance of the Handover Strategy in Chapter 7. There are various overlaps between these subjects and with other subjects, such as sustainability. Some of the points made therefore apply holistically and not just to one of these particular subjects.

What are whole life costs and why are they crucial?

Before considering whole life costs (also referred to as life cycle costs) it is crucial to consider traditional design processes, the factors that influenced the introduction of whole life costs and the cultural barriers to their integration into a holistic design process.

On the majority of projects, the Concept Design progresses once the Initial Project Brief has been agreed with the client. As part of the briefing process a Project Budget will be set and the designers, as part of their Schedule of Services, will be required to produce a design that meets this budget. This is typically achieved by the issue of regular cost estimates, usually produced by the cost consultant, as the design progresses, with the latest cost estimate signed off at the end of each stage, along with the design proposals. The cost estimate is ultimately replaced by the contractor's tender and this cost (which may not be finalised until after the building has been handed over) is typically referred to as the capital cost (or CAPex) of the building.

Cost estimate

The latest estimate for the capital cost of a building.

Capital cost (CAPex)

The CAPex or capital cost of a building is the cost of its construction, which is typically the cost agreed with the contractor and specified in the Building Contract for the construction of the project.

In recent years, it has become more commonplace for Schedules of Services to include obligations to consider whole life costs. The procurement of projects under the Private Finance Initiative (PFI) was a key driver in this trend as the contracts that were tendered included allowance for the running costs of the building for a period of time, typically 25 or 30 years. There was, therefore, a business imperative for the consortium (typically a funder, a facilities management provider and a contractor) to reduce such costs, also known as operating costs (or OPex). The sustainability agenda has provided further impetus on this subject: a building that is run more cost effectively is inevitably more beneficial in environmental terms. Many design aspects of a project can deliver reduced operating costs without increasing capital costs. However, in many instances the additional capital costs can only be justified if the payback period warrants the additional expenditure.

Operating costs (OPex)

The OPex or operating costs are the costs associated with the maintenance and operation of a building and its associated activities. The OPex and CAPex are closely related as the specification of certain aspects of the constructed building has a direct link to its running costs.

Payback period

If an item with a capital cost of £1,000 (a control panel for a boiler, for example) delivers a reduced annual running cost of £100, then its payback period is 10 years. In considering whether this capital expenditure is justified, the client needs to take this period into account. For example, if the client intends to move house in 5 years' time, they may decide that the expense is not justified. However, they may also decide that as the item will improve the house in terms of its environmental impact the costs can be justified and that they will be recouped when the house is sold on.

The whole life agenda has been driven and moved forward by owner-occupiers, who, like PFI operators, can take a view on the capital costs, particularly where an increase to the Project Budget may be required to reduce the operating costs. Conversely, the Achilles' heel in the shift towards considering operating costs is that, in many instances, the party responsible for the capital costs will not be bearing the operating costs and there is therefore no incentive for them to reduce these costs.

For example, a developer constructing an office block or shopping centre and renting the space, or constructing a block of flats and selling them on completion, has little incentive to increase the capital costs. However, sustainability legislation requires greater consideration of environmental issues and, in turn, operating costs, and as tenants or purchasers become more concerned with environmental matters and running costs, these trends will shift.

How does the RIBA Plan of Work 2013 assist consideration of whole life costs?

While the RIBA Plan of Work 2013 does not specifically include the term 'whole life costs' it encourages greater consideration of this subject and emphasises it in a number of ways.

Initial Project Brief

The Stage 1 Core Objectives require the development of Project Outcomes and the Project Budget. Both of these aspects have an influence on whole life costs, as set out below.

Project Outcomes

Financial outcomes can be core Project Outcomes. This topic is covered in the next chapter.

Project Budget and Cost Information

The Project Budget does not need to be restricted to capital costs. It might include the cost of the design fees and may also include annual maintenance fees that will be allocated when the building is in use. The capital costs themselves may be split into a number of subject headings: for example, advance utility improvements or furniture installations after the main Building Contract has been concluded. Similarly, Cost Information may comprise the latest cost estimate of the capital costs, as well as more holistic cost exercises. The scope of Cost Information and the associated advice will depend on the specific project requirements of the client and the associated services of each member of the design team.

Maintenance and Operational Strategy

The RIBA Plan of Work 2013 advocates the preparation of a Maintenance and Operational Strategy as part of the design process. As well as being a health and safety requirement, it ensures that the operating costs have been properly considered as part of the design process. In some instances, the cost consultant may be required to calculate high-level running costs based on the Maintenance and Operational Strategy. This can provide the client with greater reassurance that the developing design fits in with their long-term cost parameters.

Sustainability Strategy

This strategy is explained in greater detail in Chapter 8.

What is the relationship between whole life costs and Project Outcomes?

Savings to design and capital costs can be a false economy if those savings result in increased operating or other in-use project costs, such as the costs associated with those working in a building. This principle is illustrated in Figure 4.1, and whilst there is currently insufficient benchmarking data available to accurately illustrate the ratios between each 'circle', this figure diagrammatically makes this point. However, it is anticipated that as benchmarking initiatives grow with the increase in the use of Project Information post occupancy it is likely that this subject will be analysed in greater depth and that these ratios will be better understood. As set out in the next chapter, financial or economic costs are an important aspect of Project Outcomes.

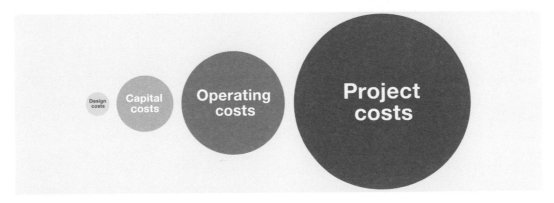

Figure 4.1 Project costs related to each aspect of the design, construction and in-use phases

Chapter

Project
Outcomes

Operating costs are, of course, just one aspect of the whole life cycle of a building and just one of a number of Project Outcomes. Project Outcomes are all those changes that take place as a direct result of a project, bringing benefits not just in relation to cost but to a number of other subjects, including social and environmental factors. It is becoming increasingly important to give full consideration to Project Outcomes and they are therefore given due prominence in the RIBA Plan of Work 2013.

The successful achievement of the Project Outcomes stated in the Initial Project Brief will be particularly obvious where a client is commissioning a new building and moving from one facility to another, as direct comparisons can be made, but it is not always so easy. Project Outcomes that might be stated in the Initial and Final Project Briefs might include:

- reduced reoffending rates in a prison

- reduced post-operative recovery times in a hospital

- better exam results in a new school, college or university

- increased footfall for a shopping centre

- an increase in borrowing in a library or increased diversity of users

- more use being made of community spaces

- an improvement in collaboration between departments, or

- better environmental performance.

From the list above it can be seen that the number of potential Project Outcomes is endless. Determining the desired Project Outcomes is an essential briefing skill and stating them in the Initial Project Brief provides added focus to the design stages as the design team considers how the Project Outcomes can be achieved. Indeed, Research and Development may be required in order to assist in the design process. For example, recent research in relation to hospitals has considered how colour influences hospital environments and how the recovery of patients and infection control are improved by single-bed patient rooms. Project Outcomes, however, must be focused: too many might mean that design activities fail to target the most important aspects, and too few could lead to opportunities to harness the design process more effectively being lost.

Well defined Project Outcomes are an essential part of a circular design process, providing Feedback to help inform future projects, and clients who undertake repeat projects understand their benefits. In these circumstances, further rigour needs to be applied as the Project Outcomes must be measurable in order to determine if they are successfully achieved and capable of being benchmarked against other similar projects to allow increasingly robust outcomes to be stated in successive briefs. Measuring also facilitates sharing of information and continual improvement.

Measuring can be objective or subjective. For example, energy usage targets can be objectively measured, whereas the success of a play space is a subjective topic, although user surveys can provide a more objective evaluation if they are carried out in both the old and the new environments. Design Quality Indicators are another example of bringing objectivity to bear on aspects of Project Outcomes and Project Performance and allowing trends or comparisons across a number of projects to be made.

Successful Project Outcomes in certain areas may be the result of a number of factors. For example, where teaching has improved in a new school (in line with the Project Outcomes stated in the Project Brief), is this improvement a result of the new environment, the quality of the new environment, the methods of a new head teacher or a combination of all three?

How does the RIBA Plan of Work 2013 encourage consideration of Project Outcomes?

There are four important activities in the RIBA Plan of Work 2013 that encourage the use of Project Outcomes as well as ensuring that, once the desired outcomes have been established, they are achieved.

Writing the Initial Project Brief

Developing Project Outcomes, as part of the briefing process during Stage 1, for inclusion in the Initial Project Brief is a core RIBA Plan of Work 2013 requirement. In determining the Project Outcomes it is essential to consider how they might become obligations that are included in professional services contracts or in the Building Contract. Whether they are contractual obligations or not will depend on how easy it is to ascertain compliance once the building has been handed over. For example, subjective topics, such as the quality of space, will be difficult to enforce contractually. Conversely, stated environmental parameters may require monitoring over a period of time before compliance can be determined.

Project Outcomes sit within three broad categories: environmental, economic and social. They might be considered in the Initial Project Brief as follows:

- Environmental: the brief would set out the key energy performance targets to be measured in the post-occupancy period once the seasonal commissioning process has been completed. These measurements will be essential as we move towards a lower carbon economy.

- Economic: as well as measuring the capital and operating costs of the completed building, the costs of the building in use will be measured. These costs might include direct staff or other costs associated with the operation of the business.

- Social: the social outcomes of a building are harder to set and even harder to measure. The key is to consider ways in which these outcomes might be measured (for example, by undertaking surveys or interviews) in order to determine the effectiveness of the design and how such metrics might be compared between similar buildings.

Review of Information Exchanges

As the design progresses, it important to review the Information Exchanges against the Project Outcomes stated in the Initial Project Brief. This is particularly important at the end of Stage 2 as it is essential that the Concept Design is aligned to any Project Outcomes stated in the Final Project Brief.

Reviewing Project Outcomes

While stating that the desired Project Outcomes provide a useful briefing tool that can be used in isolation, it is only by measuring the finished building, or output, against these outcomes that the true success of a project, regardless of any contractual obligations, can be assessed. For this process to be effective it is important to consider how each of the desired Project Outcomes will be measured. This should be carried out during the briefing stage to gain maximum benefit. Stating the means of measurement ensures greater focus during design and construction, as each party considers how their contributions will be measured post occupancy.

Considering Schedules of Services

Greater focus on Project Outcomes is a relatively new issue. It is therefore essential that when Schedules of Services are being considered the right tasks are included as part of assembling the project team to ensure that adequate fee allowances are made and to make certain that each party is able to contribute to this valuable process as necessary.

What is the relationship between value and outcomes?

Of course, the consideration of outcomes in general is not new. For some time both the RIBA and CABE have stressed the importance of considering the value of a finished project and how good design can add value to a completed project. This underlines the fact that good design is an essential component in the pursuit of better Project Outcomes.

RIBA Value Toolkit

The RIBA Value Toolkit has been developed to assist practices to articulate the benefits of well-conceived design and the value that it can add to a project. It is downloadable free to RIBA members and chartered practices. While it is a standalone tool, it is a companion to the RIBA Quality Management toolkit. The RIBA Value Toolkit references the six types of value set out in the CABE *Value Handbook*. These are:

- exchange value (economic value)

- use value

- image value

- social value

- environmental value

- cultural value.

> **CABE *Value Handbook***
>
> The CABE *Value Handbook* is a practical guide, showing how public sector organisations can get the most from the buildings and spaces in their area. It brings together essential evidence about the benefits of good design and demonstrates how a clear understanding of the different types of value created by the built environment is the key to realising its full potential (see **www.cabe.org.uk/files/the-value-handbook.pdf**).

Conclusion

In summary, Project Outcomes are an essential briefing tool for the design process. If they are properly considered they can be measured once a project has been handed over and the effectiveness of the design and construction processes can be analysed. In some instances, the Project Outcomes may be contractual and included in the Building Contract or the professional services contracts. This practice is more commonly used where the outcomes can be objectively measured. The successful consideration of whole life costs and Project Outcomes results in reduced costs to a client and, just as importantly, better social and environmental results can be achieved in parallel with these reduced costs.

Chapter

Harnessing Building Information Modelling (BIM) using the Plan

Building Information Modelling (BIM) is radically altering the way that we design buildings. While early BIM projects harnessed the potential of emerging software to create buildings with more complex geometries, the acronym BIM is now being used as a wrapper to discuss many subject matters and as a catalyst for change.

In the UK, the Government Construction Strategy (published in May 2011, see www.gov.uk/government/publications/government-construction-strategy) has provided the impetus for many current BIM initiatives. A number of pilot projects are under way and new standards and protocols are being discussed, developed and published. The emergence of BIM has to be set within a broader context: the ongoing development of internet and associated technologies which are radically altering many business models (for example, consider recent changes to publishing, the music industry and the retail sector). Economist Jeremy Rifkin's vision, in his publication *The Third Industrial Revolution*, is endorsed by the European Parliament and underlines the radical changes that are occurring.

Designers are finally reappraising their working methods. Computer-aided design (CAD) replicates the 'analogue' processes applied to the drawing board. BIM (despite its rather anonymous acronym) is championing a more revolutionary process and moving design into the 'digital' age. Although more long-winded, BIM might be better defined as 'the means of harnessing technological change and developing new ways of briefing, designing, constructing, operating and using a facility'; in other words, creating a new Plan of Work.

At first glance, particularly for those accustomed to the jargon associated with BIM, the RIBA Plan of Work 2013 may not appear to be greatly influenced by BIM. However, the RIBA Plan of Work 2013 has been conceived in a manner that works with the most progressive of BIM projects. Conversely, the RIBA Plan of Work 2013 has also been devised to accommodate the transitional phase that allows a practice or project to incrementally change their working methods from analogue to digital.

BIM Levels

Level 0 (L0)

Level 0 BIM is the use of 2D CAD files for production information; a process that the majority of design practices have used for many years. The important point to be derived from L0 is that Common Standards and processes in relation to the use of CAD failed to gain traction as the use of CAD developed.

Level 1 (L1)

Level 1 BIM acknowledges the increased use of 2D and 3D information. For architects, 3D has increasingly been used as a conceptual design tool for analysis and development of more complex geometries and for visualisation of the finished project. This form of BIM, where only one party utilises the benefits of the model, is frequently referred to as 'lonely BIM'. With L1, the use of 3D models by trade contractors also became more commonplace, with, for example, mechanical and electrical (M&E) contractors embracing BIM to enhance their design processes and to assist in the resolution of coordination issues during the design phase rather than waiting for the design to be realised on site. In terms of processes, L1 embraced the need for Common Standards to sit alongside design processes, including BS 1192:2007, *Collaborative production of architectural, engineering and construction information – Code of practice*.

Level 2 (L2)

Level 2 BIM requires the production of 3D information models by all key members of the collaborative project team. However, these models need not co-exist in a single model. By understanding and utilising BS 1192:2007, designers can ensure that each designer's model progresses in a logical manner before it is used by another designer or a designing subcontractor within the federated model (which combines the individual design team members' models). It is not anticipated that the legal, contractual or insurance issues will change for L2 but it is fair to say that L2 BIM does expose some of the deficiencies of current contractual documentation. For example, the project roles need greater consideration and the allocation of design responsibilities between the various designers and contracting parties has to be clearer. The outputs, or Information Exchanges, at each stage will also require greater definition. L2 BIM requires better integration of the design team and the designing subcontractors, with collaborative project teams adopting Common Standards under new forms of procurement that employ 'plug and play' working methods.

Level 3 (L3)

With L2 acting as the boundary between analogue and digital processes, it is likely that there will be an evolution to L3 BIM rather than a leap. The boundary between L2 and L3 will see the development of:

- early 'rough and ready' design analysis on environmental performance, minimising iterative design time

- cost models that can be quickly derived from the model using new costing interfaces

- automated checking of building models for Building Regulations compliance and/or other technical standards

- methods of analysing health and safety aspects associated with the construction and maintenance of the building in parallel with the design, and

- asset management, key performance indicators and other Feedback information aligned with intelligent briefing enabling information in the model to be developed during design and used as part of a more sophisticated handover (Soft Landings) approach and to inform and improve future projects.

Design processes will continue to be developed to their next level of refinement so that there are clear and established methods setting out how many parties can work in the same model environment at the same time. These processes will be aligned with better Schedules of Services and responsibility documents and ways of assembling the project team.

 The 2012 *BIM Overlay to the RIBA Outline Plan of Work 2007* provided a useful overview of the different levels of BIM as defined in the Bew-Richards BIM maturity diagram in Figure 6.1, and highlighted the fact that, in order to progress to L2 BIM and onwards to L3, the following were required:

- collaborative and integrated working methods and teamwork to establish closer ties between all designers on a project, including designing trade contractors

- knowledge of databases and how these can be integrated with the building model to produce a data-rich model incorporating specification, cost, time and facilities management information

- new procurement routes and forms of contracts aligned to the new working methods

- interoperability of software to enable concurrent design activities (for example, allowing environmental modelling to occur concurrently with orientation and façade studies)

- standardisation of the frequently used definitions and a rationalisation of the new terms being developed in relation to BIM, and

- use of BIM data to analyse time (4D), cost (5D) and facilities management (6D) aspects of a project.

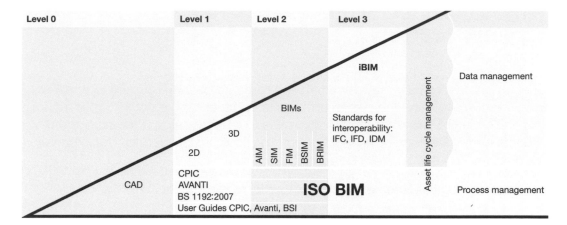

Figure 6.1 BIM maturity diagram (source: © Bew and Richards, 2008)

 The 2012 *BIM Overlay to the RIBA Outline Plan of Work 2007* also:

- noted that better briefing, including Project Outcomes, was essential

- highlighted the need for teams to be collaborative and integrated

- stressed the need to define responsibilities, Schedules of Services and organograms early in the design process

- underlined the need to refine old, and define new, project roles, particularly those related to design leadership

- acknowledged the need to identify BIM procedures and protocols

- emphasised the need to consider design responsibility

- set out the possibilities for new post-occupancy duties

- introduced the need for information drops and a delivery index (now Information Exchanges), and

- considered the importance of Construction and Design Programmes.

The RIBA Plan of Work 2013 develops these themes further. There are two core statements that set out how the RIBA Plan of Work 2013 facilitates best practice in BIM:

Better briefing processes result in more effective designs that are more focused on the client's objectives and desired Project Outcomes.

Properly assembling the project team is the backbone of a collaborative team and results in each party understanding what they have to do, when they have to do it and how it will be done.

In this chapter we consider these two topics in greater detail.

Why is the briefing process different on a BIM project?

Briefing processes vary but their aim is the same: to obtain sufficient information from the client to allow the design process to commence in a constructive manner. The RIBA Plan of Work has always acknowledged that design is iterative and that aspects of the brief may develop as design solutions are developed. The information used to develop the Concept Design may include:

- an area schedule defining the client's spatial requirements

- details of important spatial relationships (for example, between a kitchen and a dining space in a house or the waiting areas in relation to clinical spaces in a hospital)

- information on subjective themes that are important to a client (for example, the building should be 'accessible', 'light and airy', etc.)

- detailed technical requirements (for example, the number of sockets in rooms, lux levels or certain furniture or equipment to be accommodated in a room), and

- budgetary considerations.

The RIBA Plan of Work 2013 does not change these fundamental requirements. However, it does split the briefing process into two stages: the Strategic Brief related to the client's Business Case and the development of a detailed and specific Initial Project Brief.

The Strategic Brief tests the robustness of a client's Business Case and may consider refurbishment, extension and new build options or compare the merits of a number of sites before objectively recommending the best approach. It may also look at strategic cost considerations: the overall area required, benchmark costs, level of specification and any abnormal costs that might arise from a specific site. By considering the project holistically, any strategic site, briefing or cost issues can be addressed before the detail of the project is developed.

Even on a simple project, these high-level considerations can save considerable time and money on abortive design work that might result from a flawed brief.

The 3D brief

With the Strategic Brief prepared, BIM can assist in the preparation of the Initial Project Brief. Using a 3D 'block' model allows the written brief to be developed in parallel with the Feasibility Studies. The linking of the geometric model to a spreadsheet containing the areas allows iteration between the developing 3D brief and the strategic area allowances. While using a 3D model, linked to a database, to prepare the Initial Project Brief allows a more intelligent and robust brief to be prepared, there is clearly a fine line between using such a tool for briefing and the commencement of the Concept Design.

The use of the BIM model as a briefing tool is also influenced by a number of other subjects that reinforce this approach and provide clues to how BIM will change design processes.

Reuse of assemblies

Hotel chains invest considerable time in determining the size of their rooms and what they will contain, including toilets, baths, showers, storage, furniture and detailed consideration of the interior design. Modular construction is increasingly being used on these projects, with completed rooms delivered to site. Although 3D geometry is not essential for such thought processes to work, stringent Feedback from previous projects and the reuse of design information from one project to the next reinforces the circular design processes, with one project acting as a catalyst for the next.

Healthcare providers are also seeing the benefit of fixing certain aspects of a project based on previous experience. For example, an operating theatre might be reused in its entirety on a future project, right down to the light, grille, equipment and socket locations. This reuse of assemblies (typically rooms) will become more commonplace as Feedback is harnessed more effectively.

In the future, clients who undertake repeat projects will increasingly provide briefs that specify the reuse of detailed assemblies from previous projects for certain areas, along with more traditional briefing for areas where they require a project-specific design solution, for example the lobby in a hotel.

Project Outcomes

Project Outcomes also require circular processes, albeit applied in a different manner. For Project Outcomes to be successful they need to be specified in a manner that can be measured when the project is completed. More importantly, datasets from a number of similar projects are required before benchmarking can be constructively applied to a project.

The data within the BIM models and the ability to analyse this information as it is refined demonstrates how BIM can provide a significant contribution to this subject.

Post-occupancy use of design information

Designers have traditionally prepared their information solely for the purpose of constructing the building or related activities, such as gaining planning consent. While operating and maintenance manuals might be prepared, these are typically static documents. Facilities management software interfaces are being developed that will require new briefing methods to ensure that the BIM model can be effectively used for the operation of a building and not just for its construction.

These examples are not intended to be definitive. They provide suggestions as to how practices might develop their own working briefing methods and processes using the RIBA Plan of Work 2013.

How does a BIM project benefit from a well-assembled team?

The documents set out in Chapter 3 for establishing the project team have been devised, in conjunction with the RIBA Plan of Work 2013, to be applicable to any project. They have been specifically devised with a BIM project in mind. The notion is simple: if time is spent during Stage 1 considering who will be doing what, when and how, the design process will be more effective when it commences. More crucially, once the boundaries between each designer have been properly defined, any ambiguities regarding roles or duties will be removed. Furthermore, each party can proceed with confidence that their fee reflects the work they will have to undertake. As a reminder, the process defined by the documents recommended in Chapter 3 ensures that:

- the roles required on a project are properly considered

- the timing of contractor involvement is thought through

- management and design responsibilities are clear

- Information Exchanges are defined

- Project, Design and Construction Programmes are agreed, and

- project protocols are established.

The more specific aspects of this process that benefit a BIM project are:

- ensuring that it is clear which software, including the specific version, is being used by each member of the team by early completion of the Technology Strategy to be included, or referenced, in the Project Execution Plan

- agreement of the Communication Strategy and the means by which information will be distributed, commented on and developed within the project team

- agreement of the project BIM manual, determining file structuring and naming protocols

- use of the Handover Strategy to assist in the consideration of how BIM will be used during Stages 6 and 7, allowing the designers to include the relevant information within their BIM models as the design progresses

- harnessing the Design Responsibility Matrix and the Information Exchanges so that it is clear who is responsible for each aspect of the design and the level of detail required at each stage (see further below).

Properly assembling the project team is only one aspect of creating a collaborative project team. Effective communication skills are essential for a project team to be truly collaborative and, while the communication skills of individuals will be invaluable, these skills can only come into their own if the team has been properly assembled at an early stage and their processes and protocols agreed in advance of design work progressing.

How do the task bars and defined tasks in the RIBA Plan of Work 2013 benefit BIM projects?

Chapter 2 sets out the reasoning behind the eight stages and eight task bars. Five of the task bars have been conceived specifically to facilitate BIM, as detailed below.

Procurement task bar

The Procurement task bar looks at procurement holistically and considers the procurement of the project team, which includes the design team and the contractor.

Programme task bar

Collaborative contracts, such as PPC2000 (a multi-party contract published by the Association of Consultant Architects), stress the importance of having an agreed Project Programme. Generating the programme collaboratively ensures that each party in the project team is aware of the reasoning for each period. The programme is particularly important on BIM projects because greater effort is required during the early design stages. Compressed design programmes reduce crucial set-up periods or the time required to successfully iterate the design. Overlapping activities or stages with other activities, such as Stage 4 and the period during which the planning application is being considered, generate substantial risk. Generating the Project Programme ensures that it is clear who is taking such risks.

Those generating the Project Programme should bear in mind the following:

• BIM may reduce design time; however, no specific research has been published in relation to this and each practice will have to use their own experiences to make judgements regarding design periods.

• BIM may reduce the number of iterations required by the design team to coordinate the design, in particular by harnessing collaborative working.

• The need to properly set up a project team on a BIM project is vital and this period should not be compromised.

• Although BIM may reduce design time, agreeing to reduce design time creates risks for the design team. Stringent design processes are required to manage this risk and Change Control Procedures should be adopted after the Concept Design has been signed off by the client.

Suggested Key Support Tasks task bar

The purpose of the Suggested Key Support Tasks is to underline the need for certain activities to occur. In terms of BIM, agreement of the Schedules of Services, the Design Responsibility Matrix and Information Exchanges and preparation of the Project Execution Plan, including the Technology Strategy, as part of the process of assembling the project team are the most important tasks (covered in greater detail on pages 75 to 77).

Information Exchanges and UK Government Information Exchanges task bars

The Information Exchanges task bar, and the associated task bar that sets out the UK Government's Information Exchanges, play a crucial role in underlining some of the significant cultural changes required to implement BIM effectively. Information Exchanges and level of detail are considered further below.

What other aspects of the RIBA Plan of Work 2013 are crucial on a BIM project?

While all of the activities within the RIBA Plan of Work 2013 are applicable to any project, certain activities have been specially developed with BIM in mind. In particular, the Design Responsibility Matrix, Information Exchanges (and the associated level of detail) and a number of aspects related to the Project Execution Plan are of particular relevance on a BIM project.

Design Responsibility Matrix

The Design Responsibility Matrix is an important BIM document, related closely to the level of detail, which is considered further below. The Design Responsibility Matrix addresses the issue of design responsibility between consultants in the design team, but, more importantly, it also addresses the design interface between consultants and the specialist subcontractors employed by the contractor.

The boundaries between structural and building services engineers and specialist subcontractors have been clarified in recent years and there are common expectations regarding the interfaces between the various designers. For the architect, specific components, such as curtain walling, are exceptions to the rule that there is no commonly agreed method of determining those aspects for which the architect retains design responsibility and those where design responsibility passes to a specialist subcontractor via the Building Contract. JCT Building Contracts have facilitated the prescription of such elements for some time. The RIBA Plan of Work 2013, through the inclusion of specialist subcontractor design in Stage 4 and the Design Responsibility Matrix, encourages greater consideration of this important subject.

The Design Responsibility Matrix is of particular importance on a BIM project as it ensures that every party with design responsibilities is clear regarding the design information they will be contributing to the federated BIM model and the level of detail that this model will contain. The matrix is of particular importance to the lead designer, who must ensure that it allows any design coordination obligations that are allocated to this role to be undertaken.

Federated model

A holistic model of a project consisting of models from each member of the design team that are linked together – the model may contain geometric and/or data information.

Information Exchanges (and level of detail)

Chapter 3 examined why consideration of Information Exchanges is a crucial matter in relation to the RIBA Plan of Work 2013 and how use of the Information Exchanges template in assembling a collaborative project team will facilitate this. It also clarified why level of detail is an important subject.

If we consider the typical development of a federated BIM model we can begin to understand the complexities of the subject:

- The architect develops the concept design model and, following a number of iterations using rendered visualisations, achieves client sign-off.

- The structural and mechanical engineers work on their models, with the lead designer providing comments, to ensure that the concept being presented is robust.

- The iterative design process continues until all of the models are coordinated and cost-checked to confirm that the project is on budget.

- The detail of each designer's model progresses until it is sufficiently developed for use by specialist contractors to prepare their design models.

- The specialist contractors develop their models, which are checked by the lead designer, who also ensures that they integrate with the coordinated design.

- All design models are signed off and off-site manufacturing and onsite construction commence and continue until completion.

- The client or a specialist facilities management company utilises the models for the day-to-day maintenance and running of the building.

Early contractor involvement may result in a more complex interface and overlap of designers' BIM files and those prepared by specialist contractors. This scenario is based on BIM files being transferred between parties and also acting as the contractual information. The accuracy of the information in these files is therefore of paramount importance and the level of detail in each model needs to be appropriate for its purpose. Where the design baton is being handed over from designer to specialist subcontractor, the level of detail in the designer's model must be sufficient for the specialist to progress their proposals.

Protocols determining the level of detail for BIM models therefore become essential tools for use on future projects.

Project Execution Plan

A Project Execution Plan is a useful document on any project. In Chapter 3 the contents of this document were considered, and *Assembling a Collaborative Project Team* provides a further layer of information. In relation to BIM, reference is frequently made to a BIM Execution Plan or a BIM manual. The RIBA Plan of Work 2013 suggests that all of these documents are included or referenced in the Project Execution Plan. A number of aspects of the Project Execution Plan are of particular importance on a BIM project, as detailed below.

Technology Strategy

Agreement of the Technology Strategy on a project is an essential first step because different parties involved in a project team will inevitably use different software packages. Despite a move towards interchangeable data formats (IFC), outputting data from one software format into another is not always possible or is liable to data loss or corruption. Regardless of the realities or legal issues associated with these technical points, the software to be used can have a significant impact on a project. If new software has to be adopted by one party, the issues of training and working to deadlines needs to be considered, depending on the importance and complexity of the software, and additional costs for purchasing software may also have to be built into any fee proposals.

The location of hardware can also have an impact, and particularly the location of the server containing the BIM files. Is every party working from this server, which might require a high-speed internet connection? If not, how are files shared? And in what format?

In conclusion, the Technology Strategy for the project team needs to be carefully considered to ensure that each member of the team is capable of working successfully with other members and that the implications of hardware and software are considered and agreed prior to appointments being made and design work commencing.

IFC

The Industry Foundation Classes (IFC) data model is an open and freely available (i.e. not owned or managed by a single software vendor) object-based file format. It was developed by buildingSMART (formerly the International Alliance for Interoperability) to facilitate interoperability in the architecture, engineering and construction industries and is a commonly used format for BIM.

Communication Strategy

The Communication Strategy is closely related to the Technology Strategy. For example, on an international project, video conferencing (part of the Technology Strategy) may be a core communication tool.

The purpose of the Communication Strategy is to consider the interface between meetings, workshops, email, file-sharing portals, procedures for commenting on drawings and other methods used in the iterative design process. The strategy must be flexible and ad hoc meetings, calls or other methods of exchanging information will also need to be adopted.

BIM manual

The BIM manual sets out file- and drawing-naming conventions and other processes in relation to BIM. A CAD manual is typically a single-party document whereas a BIM manual has to be considered and agreed by the collaborative project team and sets out project-wide conventions and processes. Agreement of the BIM manual (or any other name by which it may be known) is a core requirement in the development of a collaborative project team.

What is meant by 'plug and play'?

Most architectural practices have their own CAD manual that sets out file- and drawing-naming conventions along with other internal CAD protocols. One of the disappointments of the CAD era is that no commonly adopted industry-wide documents or Common Standards exist (those that have been created have not been widely adopted). The concept of 'plug and play' envisages a scenario where practices can move seamlessly from one project to another and integrate collaboratively into many project teams without any changes to their internal BIM manual: an industry-wide BIM manual. The design development processes would be seamless. As project teams try to define common ways of working, the challenges in the short term will be significant. In the long term, it is likely that automated BIM processes will resolve the challenges associated with creating a 'plug and play' environment.

Conclusion

In conclusion, BIM and new digital technologies will drive cultural changes in the construction industry as we move from analogue to digital ways of working. In this guide, reference is made to how the RIBA Plan of Work 2013 facilitates a BIM project. For subjects still at an embryonic stage (level of detail, for example) we have highlighted the robustness of the RIBA Plan of Work 2013 to accommodate future change as thinking around these subjects matures.

Chapter

The changing nature of project handover

Why is Practical Completion important?

Conclusion

Handing over a building is becoming an increasingly complex process. In the period prior to handover, duties have historically been limited to administrating the Building Contract. Post handover, duties have included assisting the building user during the initial occupation period or undertaking a review of Project Performance as well as the conclusion of contract administration tasks.

The introduction of a number of new initiatives and procedures means that the post-handover period and related duties have to be considered and managed differently and acknowledged earlier in the design process. Before looking at these, it is essential to consider the importance of Practical Completion and to address some of the issues that arise from the completion of a building and its handover to the client.

Why is Practical Completion important?

Practical Completion is an important point in a project for two reasons. From the client's perspective, it is the point when possession of the completed building can take place and the building can be occupied for use. From the contractor's perspective, the granting of Practical Completion triggers a number of aspects of the contract, including the release of retention and the transfer of insurance obligations and it is the date beyond which certain damages cannot be claimed. These issues are covered in greater detail in publications such as *Law in Practice: The RIBA Legal Handbook*.

While the handover process should theoretically be straightforward, in practice it can be fraught. For example, if the contractor is running late, a request to hand over the building before the contract administrator is satisfied that it is 'practically complete' might be made in order to limit any damages. Conversely, a client may have to move from one building to another or may have other reasons why the completion date in the Building Contract is a business imperative, or partial posession and a phased handover may create contractual and operational complexities. While programme contingencies should have been allocated in the Project Programme, these may already have been utilised, creating pressure all round.

There is no firm definition of 'practically complete'. Case law suggests that it means not 100 per cent complete and, while many contractors aim for 'zero defects' at handover, it is inevitable that a number of defects, or snagging, will remain. This is particularly the case on design and build projects where the transfer of risk makes it difficult for the contractor to apply for extensions of time. A project must certainly have a certificate of completion granted before it can be handed over and compliance with health and safety requirements would form a necessary part of this process. Otherwise, the acceptable degree of incomplete work or snagging may depend on how crucial handover is to the client. Put another way, the client's need to have beneficial occupation can blur the Practical Completion process.

Aside from completion of the built works, there are several new subjects that increasingly influence this handover process. These are detailed below.

Intelligent building systems

Many buildings now contain a number of intelligent building services systems. While such systems can result in a building that has reduced whole life costs, and one that is a better building in environmental terms, such systems:

- have to be commissioned to ensure that they are running effectively and as specified and designed

- require explanation and training in order to be run effectively

- need operating manuals to be prepared to set out longer term requirements and for reference after training

- may need to be monitored to ensure compliance with contractual parameters, or Project Outcomes, for environmental performance, and

- need fine tuning, including seasonal commissioning, in order to work as designed.

All of these activities must be considered, planned and integrated into the Project and Construction Programmes so that the expectations of each member of the project team are clear. For example, there is no point in a contractor achieving what they believe to be Practical Completion if the building services do not work as planned or the users have still not been trained in how to successfully run the services installations.

While the considerations listed above primarily impact larger projects, on smaller projects more efficient environmental controls are being specified more frequently and certain passive solar devices may need explanation if they are to work effectively. The principles set out will therefore increasingly apply to smaller projects.

A further complexity is introduced where the client for a building is not the end user. This creates a further break in continuity between design and construction processes and the ultimate user of the building, who may have the greatest interest in the functionality of the building systems.

Asset management

The ability of the client to utilise the building information model or, more likely, the federated model (see Chapter 6) creates new opportunities for all of those involved in the design and construction of a building. The most fundamental shift is that the design work that is produced by the design team has historically been used solely for construction or for development by designing subcontractors whereas, moving forward, it will increasingly be used beyond construction for the operation and maintenance of the building. Of course, verifying or matching the 'drawn' information to the completed building is just the beginning of new processes that will harness and utilise the initial design for long-term maintenance and operational objectives.

'As-constructed' Information

Requests for design team members to produce 'as-built' drawings at the end of a project can lead to protracted discussions because these designers do not necessarily have detailed and specific knowledge of what was actually constructed in order to verify such a status. However, if the client is to utilise information after Practical Completion, new ways of verifying such information will be required. 'As-constructed' Information is the term used in the RIBA Plan of Work 2013.

Of greater interest is the information contained in the model. Clients, and in particular the UK Government, are increasingly requesting that models be delivered electronically at handover in formats suitable for integration into CAFM (computer-aided facility management) systems. COBie is one such format and the UK Government's current preferred means for achieving this objective. These formats are designed to ensure the incremental development of information in the model as greater definition of the design occurs at each stage and as products and components are finalised and their operational and maintenance information defined. As CAFM systems become more commonly used, the requirement to provide such information at handover will increase.

COBie

The Construction Operations Building information exchange (COBie) is a life cycle information exchange format that describes the spaces and equipment within a facility. BIM software is utilised to export COBie data during the design process (Information Exchanges). At project handover the information can be imported into any CAFM system used by the client, end user or facilities manager. When kept updated, such a system ensures that the accuracy of the BIM information is maintained.

Project Outcomes

The benefits of Project Outcomes have already been set out in Chapter 5. In the context of Practical Completion it is important to remember that certain Project Outcomes may be a contractual imperative and that others may require measurement or analysis to allow a client to provide an informed brief on a future project. The Handover Strategy should set out any requirements so that Schedules of Services can be agreed accordingly and adequate allowances made in the Project Budget if these services are not commissioned at the start of the project.

Benchmarking

As more data becomes available on completed projects it will become easier to assess and compare different projects, particularly where the data can be objectively compared (for example, comparing the amount of energy used on a number of buildings). For benchmarking to be implemented accurately, information will have to be recorded at the end of a project and the need for this task to be undertaken included in Schedules of Services. More importantly, benchmarking exercises will have to be implemented during the briefing stage so that realistic targets are set prior to design work commencing.

Conclusion

In summary, handing over a building requires a number of activities to take place prior to Practical Completion or occupation of the building. Traditionally, the handover process has related to the completion of the built works. However, a number of subjects now need to be considered and planned.

Once the building is in use, the information produced by the designers may be used for the management of the building (or asset). Other activities, to fine tune the building or to ensure that the building is being used as anticipated, might be required. Project Outcomes may need to be measured and reviewed and other post-occupancy exercises undertaken. These activities are varied: many need to be considered at the outset of a project to ensure that the design process delivers the briefed requirements and to make sure that adequate fee allowances are made for undertaking these tasks.

While the RIBA Plan of Work 2013 advocates the preparation of a draft Handover Strategy at Stage 1, to allow all of the tasks to be considered while the project team is being assembled, it is important to remember that it is the Schedules of Services and other contractual documents which determine the actual services to be undertaken by the project team with respect to handover and in-use activities.

Soft Landings

The Building Services Research and Information Association or BSRIA **(www.bsria.co.uk)** and the Usable Buildings Trust **(www.usablebuildings.co.uk)** have developed the Soft Landings Framework over a number of years. Further information can be accessed at **www.bsria.co.uk/news/soft-landings-framework/**.

Government Soft Landings (GSL)

The GSL framework is reflective of work that has been undertaken by BSRIA and the Usable Buildings Trust in their development of Soft Landings. The UK Government Construction Strategy aimed to improve public sector construction and contribute to both growth and efficiency savings by a number of means. A key area identified was the need to align design and construction with operational asset management, and encourage increased use of outcome-based specifications against clear performance criteria. GSL has been developed in order to meet these requirements (see **www.bimtaskgroup.org/gsl-policy**). The reason for the creation of an asset and its intended business purpose, or the 'golden thread', can often be lost in the construction process. GSL will be used to maintain this 'golden thread' and ensure its continuation into the building's operative stage. In particular, it will focus on the following:

- ensuring that GSL is implemented as standard for government projects

- early engagement during the design process with end users, clients and facilities managers

- continuing post-construction responsibility for the project on the part of the design and construction teams

- implementing a contractual mechanism to ensure the above

- establishing an appropriate handover process from construction to end user or facilities manager

- Post-occupancy Evaluation or monitoring and tie back to ownership and lessons learned for future design.

Guidance will be presented in the form of BIM process maps to take projects through the four required areas of:

- *environmental performance*: each project will have an environmental performance plan at the core of the design brief

- *building management*: there will be a clear, cost-efficient vision and strategy for managing the facilities

- *commissioning, training and handover*: the building will be delivered and handed over through a plan specifically designed to meet the needs of the end users, building managers, facilities managers and occupiers

- *performance effectiveness and efficiency*: facilities must be designed to meet the needs of the project sponsor and occupiers and provide an effective, productive working environment.

Chapter

Sustainability

Integrating sustainability into the RIBA Plan of Work 2013 has been a core objective. This chapter summarises the sustainability aims at each stage, linked to corresponding Sustainability Checkpoints, and supplementary notes that encourage the review of relevant sustainability issues as a project progresses.

Establishing the Sustainability Aspirations of a client is a crucial starting point. It sets the sustainability context for the project and can have a significant impact on the processes of briefing, setting a budget and Project Programme, selecting a procurement strategy, including assembling the appropriate project team, and defining the architectural design approach, coordinated services strategy and other services that may be required. The approach will vary significantly between different projects and clients. Some clients will have highly developed Sustainability Aspirations, policies and targets that can be directly transposed into the brief whereas, for less experienced or aware clients, more direct input by the design team may be needed to raise awareness of relevant issues and help to clarify their ambitions and any particular approaches that they may wish to adopt. The client's Sustainability Aspirations may include a mix of objective and subjective aspects, such as:

- measures or specific levels of performance defined by recognised third party standards

- specific requirements in relation to operational or facilities management issues

- particular requirements for resilience to projected changes in the climate

- the ability to accommodate changes of use in future, and

- a requirement to minimise a new building's embodied carbon or energy.

Chapter 5 outlined the role and importance of the Initial Project Brief in achieving the desired Project Outcomes. In a similar vein, the need to properly consider and embed the Sustainability Aspirations into the Initial Project Brief is essential if the design is to embrace and respond to these objectives. As the Concept Design stage progresses, design proposals should be reviewed against the Sustainability Aspirations for inclusion in the Final Project Brief. If an integrated sustainable building is to be achieved, it is essential that a balanced and structured review of these aspirations is complete prior to defining and finalising the Initial Project Brief.

For a building to be truly sustainable it must deliver the good intentions that are embedded in its design once it is occupied, and then continue to do so throughout its life. In order to do this effectively, throughout the briefing, design, construction and handover processes particular attention should be paid to how the building will be operated and maintained.

The Sustainability Checkpoints and supplementary notes include examples of behaviours and activities that will assist this process, including:

- specifically involving in the briefing process those who will use and operate the building

- learning from previous projects in order to set realistic and measurable targets

- carrying out reality checks through the design and construction process

- implementing an enhanced handover process with the option of monitoring and aftercare services once the building is occupied.

This approach has been embraced by the UK Government as 'Government Soft Landings' (see page 84), which is anticipated to become a requirement for all public procurement by 2016. Further information on the concept is set out in BSRIA's Soft Landings Framework (see page 83).

In the sections below, the aims of the Sustainability Strategy at each RIBA stage are stated, along with the Sustainability Checkpoints highlighted in a bespoke RIBA Plan of Work 2013 created using the online tool. These Sustainability Checkpoints are designed to provide members of the project team with an overview of the most important sustainability tasks that should be undertaken at each stage and a means of ensuring that they have been carried out. The supplementary notes provide a list of additional supporting activities that can be used in the development of the Sustainability Strategy.

Stage 0 – Strategic Definition

Sustainability aims

Establish the client's Sustainability Aspirations so that these can be properly taken into account in developing the Strategic Brief and Business Case.

Checkpoints

- Ensure that a strategic sustainability review of client needs and potential sites has been carried out, including reuse of existing facilities, building components or materials.

Supplementary notes

- This 'awareness' stage sets the sustainability context for the project.

- Review client requirements to distil their Sustainability Aspirations and the expected building lifespan against which capital costs and costs in use should be balanced.

- The client should consider appointing or identifying a client sustainability advocate (in a senior management position) and/or appointing a sustainability champion within the project team.

- Assess environmental opportunities and constraints of potential sites and building assets, including sufficient iterative modelling to support the conclusions of any Feasibility Studies.

- Initial consultation with stakeholders, identification of local planning sustainability requirements and appraisal of existing building, social, transportation, water, energy, ecological and renewable resources, including the need for pre-construction or seasonal monitoring or surveys, should be undertaken.

- Identify potential funding sources and their eligibility criteria.

- Review relevant current and emerging EU, national and local sustainability policies and legislation and analyse their implications for building, environmental and performance targets.

- Identify and understand the final occupants' needs in order to help to establish user patterns, energy profiles and the performance standards required.

- Obtain a letter from the planning authority to verify any sustainability requirements.

Stage 1 – Preparation and Brief

Sustainability aims

During Stage 1, the Sustainability Aspirations should be considered and included in the Initial Project Brief, defining criteria to be met as appropriate. A budget, procurement route and design process should be established that will promote the realisation of those aspirations and a project team with the required resources, skills and commitment assembled.

Checkpoints

- Confirm that formal sustainability targets are stated in the Initial Project Brief.

- Confirm that environmental requirements, building lifespan and future climate parameters are stated in the Initial Project Brief.

- Have early stage consultations, surveys or monitoring been undertaken as necessary to meet sustainability criteria or assessment procedures?

- Check that the principles of the Handover Strategy and post-completion services are included in each party's Schedule of Services.

- Confirm that the Site Waste Management Plan has been implemented.

Supplementary notes

- Commission surveys of existing buildings to be retained (including condition, historic/townscape significance, materials and components for recycling), services, noise, vibration, renewable energy resources, ecology, geology, etc. as required to inform the brief.

- Review options for formal assessment of aspects of sustainability and/or energy performance (e.g. BREEAM, LEED, Passivhaus). If the project is a component of a larger scheme, ensure that targets support and are consistent with any overarching sustainability assessment methodologies. Establish a timetable for associated assessor appointment and early stage actions.

- Include a simple description in the Initial Project Brief of the internal environmental conditions that the client requires.

- Involve the client's facilities management team and review past experience (both good and bad) in a spirit of openness in order to set environmental and performance targets or Project Outcomes that are useful, measurable and challenging but achievable and unambiguous. Energy use and carbon emissions targets should include both regulated and unregulated use.

- Agree how to measure performance in use, what incentives there will be to achieve Project Outcomes and what action is appropriate if anything falls short.

- Develop potential energy strategies, including estimated energy demand calculations, options for renewables and implications for building or site design (e.g. whether there is sufficient plant space).

- Develop water efficiency strategies to establish similarly robust performance targets.

- Set out sustainable drainage systems (SuDS) and surface water retention requirements.

- Develop a brief for specialist environmental sub-consultants (e.g. wind monitoring consultants, ecologists).

- Consider climate change adaptation criteria and future performance standards.

- Set out any future uses or reconfiguration to be accommodated.

- Ensure that the competence of potential design team members matches the client's Sustainability Aspirations.

- Client to implement the Site Waste Management Plan to enable designers to record decisions made to reduce waste as the project progresses.

Stage 2 – Concept Design

Sustainability aims

To develop a Concept Design that embodies the underpinning Sustainability Aspirations of the project with sufficient detail and analysis to be confident that key strategies can be delivered in practice.

Checkpoints

- Confirm that formal sustainability pre-assessment and identification of key areas of design focus have been undertaken and that any deviation from the Sustainability Aspirations has been reported and agreed.

- Has the initial Building Regulations Part L assessment been carried out?

- Have 'plain English' descriptions of internal environmental conditions and seasonal control strategies and systems been prepared?

- Has the environmental impact of key materials and the Construction Strategy been checked?

- Has resilience to future changes in climate been considered?

Supplementary notes

- Set out the site-scale environmental design criteria (e.g. solar orientation, overshadowing, SuDS, waste).

- Consider the design of the space between buildings as well as the buildings themselves.

- Consider the need for and scale of private, semi-private and public external space.

- Establish maximum plan depths to achieve desired levels of natural ventilation, daylight and view.

- Design for buildability, usability and manageability.

- Consider the impact of complexity of form on thermal performance, airtightness and inefficient or wasteful use of materials.

- Establish an appropriate glazing proportion and shading strategy for each orientation to provide good levels of daylight while avoiding excessive glare, solar gain or heat loss.

- Establish appropriate element thicknesses to achieve the U-values required by the energy strategy.

- Check that materials and the construction approach will provide a level of thermal mass that is appropriate to the environmental design strategy.

- Refine and review design decisions to minimise the quantity of materials used and to minimise construction waste (for guidance, see www.wrap.org.uk/designingoutwaste).

- Review the embodied impacts of the materials and the construction approach in the context of the building's lifespan.

- Avoid design solutions that inhibit adaptation and alternative use of the building or its components and materials.

- Take particular care to avoid short- and long-term damage to retained traditional building fabric from ill-considered upgrade interventions.

- Ensure that the design implications of any components, essential to the success of the Sustainability Strategy (e.g. space for fuel deliveries and waste handling, roof collector area and orientation, location and size of rainwater harvesting tanks, SuDS attenuation, etc.) are understood by all members of the project team.

- Refine the energy and servicing strategy, incorporating energy-efficient services design and design techniques.

- Carry out sufficient compliance or advanced modelling to prove the design concept before freezing the design (e.g. SBEM/SAP/PHPP (Passivhaus Planning Package) or dynamic modelling).

- Audit the emerging design against the project's Sustainability Strategy and Project Outcomes.

- Set up a programme of intermediate evaluations and reality checks involving stakeholders and key users as well as the design team.

Stage 3 – Developed Design

Sustainability aims

To ensure that the Developed Design reflects the underpinning Sustainability Strategy.

Checkpoints

- Has a full formal sustainability assessment been carried out?

- Have an interim Building Regulations Part L assessment and a design stage carbon/energy declaration been undertaken?

- Has the design been reviewed to identify opportunities to reduce resource use and waste and the results recorded in the Site Waste Management Plan?

Supplementary notes

- Refine and distil the project's Sustainability Strategy, checking against brief and targets.

- Update energy modelling as the design develops and check against targets.

- Refine the climate adaptation strategy and make provision for future adaptation interventions.

- Incorporate environmental and sustainability issues in the Planning Application Design and Access Statement, including a development of the Stage 2 'plain English' description of internal environmental conditions, seasonal control strategy and systems. Provide a supplementary detailed report if appropriate.

- Consider peer reviews of environmental control strategies and also involve stakeholders and users.

- Instigate initial involvement of and advice to contractors and specialist subcontractors where specialist products or systems are proposed.

- Audit the Developed Design to ensure integration and compliance with the project's sustainability targets.

Stage 4 – Technical Design

Sustainability aims

To ensure that the final design work prepared by the design team and the follow-on design work by specialist subcontractors reflects the technical requirements of the underpinning Sustainability Strategy.

Checkpoints

- Is the formal sustainability assessment substantially complete?

- Have details been audited for airtightness and continuity of insulation?

- Has the Building Regulations Part L submission been made and the design stage carbon/energy declaration been updated and the future climate impact assessment prepared?

- Has a non-technical user guide been drafted and have the format and content of the Part L log book been agreed?

- Has all outstanding design stage sustainability assessment information been submitted?

- Are building Handover Strategy and monitoring technologies specified?

- Have the implications of changes to the specification or design been reviewed against agreed sustainability criteria?

- Has compliance of agreed sustainability criteria for contributions by specialist subcontractors been demonstrated?

Supplementary notes

- Agree technical requirements to support the monitoring strategy.

- Ensure that artificial lighting and daylighting strategies and controls are mutually supportive in delivering low energy consumption.

- Involve facilities management and users in reviewing the environmental control systems and manual and automatic controls to ensure that they are appropriately simple and intuitive, and that there is a match between expectations and the design.

- Make sure that the project team is aware of the technical consequences of strategic sustainability decisions.

- Specify sustainable materials and products, balancing life-cycle assessment, maintenance regime, durability and cost.

- Complete consultation with subcontractors and suppliers with regard to Technical Design issues and review information packages to check that they are coordinated, complementary and support all components of the Sustainability Strategy.

- Agree responsibilities and routines for data recording to monitor performance.

- Review the potential knock-on implications of value engineering on performance and sustainability targets.

- Review the final details, including subcontractors' packages, for airtightness and continuity of insulation.

- Review the information required to demonstrate compliance with sustainability requirements (e.g. materials certification).

Stage 5 – Construction

Sustainability aims

To ensure that the Sustainability Strategy underpinning the design is carried through into construction and to manage the handover in a way that will ensure that the client can operate the building as intended on occupation.

Checkpoints

- Has the design stage sustainability assessment been certified?

- Have sustainability procedures been developed with the contractor and included in the Construction Strategy?

- Has the detailed commissioning and Handover Strategy programme been reviewed?

- Confirm that the contractor's interim testing and monitoring of construction has been reviewed and observed, particularly in relation to airtightness and continuity of insulation.

- Is the non-technical user guide complete and the aftercare service set up?

- Has the 'As-constructed' Information been issued for post-construction sustainability certification?

Supplementary notes

- Collaborate with the contractor to maximise construction phase potential to meet sustainability criteria as economically as possible.

- Submit final information for statutory approval and certification including Building Regulations Part L submission and energy performance certificates (EPC).

- Visit the site to check that quality, installation, etc. is in line with sustainability targets.

- Review the content of the operating and maintenance manual with the facilities manager, who should sign it off when it is complete and acceptable. Stress the importance of design elements that are essential to meeting sustainability targets and how to monitor whether they are operating correctly.

- Work with the client's facilities managers to ensure a smooth handover, with all records finalised and coordinated and with adequately trained operating and maintenance staff in place in advance of completion.

- Check that adequate maintenance contracts are in place and that they will commence immediately after handover.

- Confirm responsibilities and routines for data recording to monitor performance and assist in fine tuning.

- Identify aftercare representative(s) and when they will be available on site.

- Refer to the Handover Strategy for detailed guidance on preparations to be made for handover and post-completion activities.

Stage 6 – Handover and Close Out

Sustainability aims

To support the client in the early stages of occupation and to provide aftercare services as agreed.

Checkpoints

- Has assistance with the collation of post-completion information for final sustainability certification been provided?

Supplementary notes

- If necessary, review the project sustainability features and operation methods with the client, facilities managers and occupants.

- Assist with the fine tuning of building services and operational systems to check that they meet user requirements.

Stage 7 – In Use

Sustainability aims

To provide any services relevant to the operation or use of the building as agreed.

Checkpoints

- Has observation of the building operation in use and assistance with fine tuning and guidance for occupants been undertaken?

- Has the energy/carbon performance been declared?

Supplementary notes

- Review controls and performance in each season and update manuals and records to reflect any change.

- Feedback lessons learned from the post-occupancy review to the client and project team.

Conclusion

The aspects of sustainability covered in the RIBA Plan of Work 2013 are not comprehensive; however, sufficient seeds are sown to ensure that the requisite strategies are prepared in response to the Sustainability Aspirations that are established at the outset of the project. Furthermore, the RIBA Plan of Work 2013 aims to ensure that each subject is considered in its proper order as the design progresses and, just as importantly, that the commissioning, handover and post-handover activities are adequately scoped at the outset to ensure that the building in use operates effectively and as designed.

Chapter

Enhancing health
and safety

Addressing health and safety is a core requirement on any project and is backed by substantial legislation. However, the RIBA Plan of Work 2013 does not make specific reference to statutory legislation regarding health and safety for a number of reasons:

- Legislation changes – avoiding specific references eliminates the need to alter the RIBA Plan of Work if there are any changes to statutory legislation.

- Other statutory legislation, such as the Planning Acts and Building Regulations, is not referenced in the RIBA Plan of Work 2013.

- Legislation typically represents a minimum legal requirement.

- Limiting safety aspects to complying with legislation does not encourage the use of innovative approaches or harness progress made in approaches that raise health and safety standards.

- Reference to health and safety legislation could only be made in summary form, which would not encourage consideration of the subject in a detailed holistic manner.

Project roles

The RIBA Plan of Work 2013 embraces health and safety issues by clearly defining each project role. Providing health and safety advice is a core obligation of any professional role. Legislative requirements to manage this process are fulfilled by the health and safety adviser, who ensures that any legislative duties and requirements are carried out by the project team. As a key adviser to the client, those undertaking the role are also encouraged to consider other health and safety initiatives as part of a project Health and Safety Strategy and to contribute to the development of the Risk Assessment process, the Maintenance and Operational Strategy and, where appropriate, the Construction Strategy. These must all consider health and safety in a proportionate, practical and holistic manner.

Each party undertaking a specific role or roles might also have a duty to comply with other aspects of health and safety legislation. As noted above, these requirements are not stated in the RIBA Plan of Work 2013 as they may change from time to time. However, the Health and Safety Strategy would certainly include Risk Assessments and some of the other strategies set out below to aid compliance with such requirements.

Risk Assessments

The RIBA Plan of Work 2013 advocates the use of appropriate tools arising from UK Government and EU legislation, including the preparation and review of Risk Assessments throughout the design process to assist with the elimination, reduction and management of health and safety issues as the design and construction progresses. Risk Assessments, and other proactive measures, are instrumental in applying holistic and practical controls during the design, procurement, construction and operation phases of a project.

For Risk Assessments to be successful, each party should develop their own analysis of the specific health and safety issues within the project. It is then essential that all the risks associated with the project as a whole are collated, recorded and circulated to the project team. The lead designer may be required to ensure that the collated risks associated with design are passed on to the relevant parties during the procurement and construction phases.

Maintenance and Operational Strategy

The Maintenance and Operational Strategy performs a number of functions. It allows the design team to demonstrate how a building can be maintained and operated on handover and, as part of this process, ensures that the 'base' building includes all of the measures required to comply with the strategy (for example, is there a garage or storeroom for cleaning equipment?). Producing the strategy also confirms the fact that the health and safety aspects of post-occupancy activities have been considered and contributes to reducing operational costs.

The Maintenance and Operational Strategy not only sets the maintenance regime but requires any health and safety aspects to be identified and controlled or eliminated during the design process. This ensures that the client is aware of and understands any residual risks that will carry over into the operational phase (for example, the operational implications of a specific method proposed for window cleaning).

Construction Strategy

The Construction Strategy should be developed by the construction lead. However, it is important to consider buildability during the early project stages and the contractor's ability to contribute to this process will depend on when they become involved.

Where the contractor is appointed after Stage 2, the duties in the early stages may be carried out by the lead designer, by another member of the design team or by a specialist consultant, depending on the composition of the design team and the specific complexities of the project prior to the contractor's involvement. In any case, the Construction Strategy would be prepared collaboratively with contributions from each design team member taken into consideration. When the contractor becomes involved they take over responsibility for the Construction Strategy, with any major deviations in strategy considered during the tender phase. Put another way, the document is a core health and safety tool that requires consideration of the construction process as a whole with specific and particular attention paid to buildability from the early design stages.

On larger projects the Construction Strategy would ensure that details of aspects such as site logistics, cranage, site access and similar decisions are incrementally and proportionately included as the project progresses. Some aspects of the Construction Strategy, such as how to deal with an underpinned boundary wall, for example, will be derived from the design process; others may be determined during the tender process, when the contractor is calculating the preliminary costs, such as site cabin locations, cranage strategies and other logistical issues. The contractor will ultimately be the focus of this strategy; however, the design team will be instrumental in setting out aspects of the design that require specific attention during the construction period.

On smaller projects, it is likely that the architect would develop the Construction Strategy for inclusion with the tender documents issued to the contractor. On these projects, the Construction Strategy can also be useful and can help to minimise queries or problems arising on site. For example, in the case of a small first floor flat conversion with a steep and narrow existing staircase, consideration would need to be given to the delivery of materials (a new bath or a large, heavy door, for example).

The Construction Strategy might also advocate that all works are registered with the Considerate Constructors Scheme to provide a further layer of health and safety monitoring on a project. This scheme also assists in the development of sustainability measures during the construction process.

Considerate Constructors Scheme

The Considerate Constructors Scheme is the national initiative set up by the construction industry to improve its image. Construction sites and companies that register with the Scheme are monitored against a Code of Considerate Practice, designed to encourage best practice beyond statutory requirements. The Scheme's remit covers any aspect of construction activity that might have a direct or indirect impact on the image of the industry as a whole. The main areas of concern fall into three categories: the general public, the workforce and the environment. For full details, visit the Scheme's website: **www.ccscheme.org.uk**.

Health and Safety Strategy

The main purpose of the Health and Safety Strategy is to set out how compliance with legislation is to be achieved. However, it would also be used to capture other health and safety initiatives on a project and encourage the adoption of industry best practice rather than simply compliance with minimum legal requirements. The Health and Safety Strategy can be developed by the health and safety adviser and it may be initiated in a workshop environment with the collaborative project team.

The Health and Safety Strategy may be derived from a template that is adapted to suit changing legislative requirements and amended to include the particular aims of a practice or client.

Handover Strategy

The Handover Strategy deals with the many aspects associated with handing over a building and other post-occupancy activities. The Handover Strategy would need to consider any health and safety issues associated with phased handovers.

Conclusion

An essential component of any Feedback processes would be consideration of the Health and Safety Strategy and how this might be improved and developed on future projects. The Construction Strategy can also be reviewed to determine whether it would have been productive for the designers to have considered certain construction aspects earlier in the design process.

In conclusion, health and safety is imbedded into the RIBA Plan of Work 2013 in a manner that encourages consideration of best practice in relation to health and safety for all aspects of a project, including the operational and maintenance periods.

10

Terms used throughout the RIBA Plan of Work 2013

A number of new themes and subject matters have been included in the RIBA Plan of Work 2013. This chapter presents a glossary of all of the capitalised terms that are used throughout the RIBA Plan of Work 2013. Defining certain terms has been necessary to clarify the intent of a term, to provide additional insight into the purpose of certain terms and to ensure consistency in the interpretation of the RIBA Plan of Work 2013.

Term / task	Definition
'As-constructed' Information	Information produced at the end of a project to represent what has been constructed. This will comprise a mixture of 'as-built' information from specialist subcontractors and the 'final construction issue' from design team members. Clients may also wish to undertake 'as-built' surveys using new surveying technologies to bring a further degree of accuracy to this information.
Building Contract	The contract between the client and the contractor for the construction of the project. In some instances, the Building Contract may contain design duties for specialist subcontractors and/or design team members. On some projects, more than one Building Contract may be required, for example one for shell and core works and another for furniture, fitting and equipment aspects.
Building Information Modelling (BIM)	BIM is widely used as the acronym for Building Information Modelling, which is commonly defined (using the Construction Project Information Committee (CPIC) definition) as: 'digital representation of physical and functional characteristics of a facility creating a shared knowledge resource for information about it and forming a reliable basis for decisions during its life cycle, from earliest conception to demolition'.
Business Case	The Business Case for a project is the rationale behind the initiation of a new building project. It may consist solely of a reasoned argument. It may contain supporting information, financial appraisals or other background information. It should also highlight initial considerations for the Project Outcomes. In summary, it is a combination of objective and subjective considerations. The Business Case might be prepared in relation to, for example, appraising a number of sites or in relation to assessing a refurbishment against a new build option.

Change Control Procedures	Procedures for controlling change to the design and construction following the sign-off of the Stage 2 Concept Design and the Final Project Brief.
Common Standards	Publicly available standards frequently used to define project and design management processes in relation to the briefing, designing, constructing, maintaining, operating and use of a building.
Communication Strategy	The strategy that sets out when the project team will meet, how they will communicate effectively and the protocols for issuing information between the various parties, both informally and at Information Exchanges.
Construction Programme	The period in the Project Programme and the Building Contract for the construction of the project, commencing on the site mobilisation date and ending at Practical Completion.
Construction Strategy	A strategy that considers specific aspects of the design that may affect the buildability or logistics of constructing a project, or may affect health and safety aspects. The Construction Strategy comprises items such as cranage, site access and accommodation locations, reviews of the supply chain and sources of materials, and specific buildability items, such as the choice of frame (steel or concrete) or the installation of larger items of plant. On a smaller project, the strategy may be restricted to the location of site cabins and storage, and the ability to transport materials up an existing staircase.
Contractor's Proposals	Proposals presented by a contractor to the client in response to a tender that includes the Employer's Requirements. The Contractor's Proposals may match the Employer's Requirements, although certain aspects may be varied based on value engineered solutions and additional information may be submitted to clarify what is included in the tender. The Contractor's Proposals form an integral component of the Building Contract documentation.
Contractual Tree	A diagram that clarifies the contractual relationship between the client and the parties undertaking the roles required on a project.

Cost Information	All of the project costs, including the cost estimate and life cycle costs where required.
Design Programme	A programme setting out the strategic dates in relation to the design process. It is aligned with the Project Programme but is strategic in its nature, due to the iterative nature of the design process, particularly in the early stages.
Design Queries	Queries relating to the design arising from the site, typically managed using a contractor's in-house request for information (RFI) or technical query (TQ) process.
Design Responsibility Matrix	A matrix that sets out who is responsible for designing each aspect of the project and when. This document details the extent of any Performance Specified Design. The Design Responsibility Matrix is created at a strategic level at Stage 1 and fine tuned in response to the Concept Design at the end of Stage 2 in order to ensure that there are no design responsibility ambiguities at Stages 3, 4 and 5.
Employer's Requirements	Proposals prepared by design team members. The level of detail will depend on the stage at which the tender is issued to the contractor. The Employer's Requirements may comprise a mixture of prescriptive elements and descriptive elements to allow the contractor a degree of flexibility in determining the Contractor's Proposals.
Feasibility Studies	Studies undertaken on a given site to test the feasibility of the Initial Project Brief on a specific site or in a specific context and to consider how site-wide issues will be addressed.
Feedback	Feedback from the project team, including the end users, following completion of a building.
Final Project Brief	The Initial Project Brief amended so that it is aligned with the Concept Design and any briefing decisions made during Stage 2. (Both the Concept Design and Initial Project Brief are Information Exchanges at the end of Stage 2.)

Handover Strategy	The strategy for handing over a building, including the requirements for phased handovers, commissioning, training of staff or other factors crucial to the successful occupation of a building. On some projects, the Building Services Research and Information Association (BSRIA) Soft Landings process is used as the basis for formulating the strategy and undertaking a Post-occupancy Evaluation (see www.bsria.co.uk/services/design/soft-landings/).
Health and Safety Strategy	The strategy covering all aspects of health and safety on the project, outlining legislative requirements as well as other project initiatives, including the Maintenance and Operational Strategy.
Information Exchange	The formal issue of information for review and sign-off by the client at key stages of the project. The project team may also have additional formal Information Exchanges as well as the many informal exchanges that occur during the iterative design process.
Initial Project Brief	The brief prepared following discussions with the client to ascertain the Project Objectives, the client's Business Case and, in certain instances, in response to site Feasibility Studies.
Maintenance and Operational Strategy	The strategy for the maintenance and operation of a building, including details of any specific plant required to replace worn out building services and other building components.
Post-occupancy Evaluation	Evaluation undertaken post occupancy to determine whether the Project Outcomes, both subjective and objective, set out in the Final Project Brief have been achieved.
Practical Completion	Practical Completion is a contractual term used in the Building Contract to signify the date on which a project is handed over to the client. The date triggers a number of contractual mechanisms.

Project Budget	The client's budget for the project, which may include the construction cost as well as the cost of certain items required post completion and during the project's operational use.
Project Execution Plan	The Project Execution Plan is produced in collaboration between the project lead and lead designer, with contributions from other designers and members of the project team. The Project Execution Plan sets out the processes and protocols to be used to develop the design. It is sometimes referred to as a project quality plan.
Project Information	Information, including models, documents, specifications, schedules and spreadsheets, issued between parties during each stage and in formal Information Exchanges at the end of each stage.
Project Objectives	The client's key objectives as set out in the Initial Project Brief. The document includes, where appropriate, the employer's Business Case, Sustainability Aspirations or other aspects that may influence the preparation of the brief and, in turn, the Concept Design stage. For example, Feasibility Studies may be required in order to test the Initial Project Brief against a given site, allowing certain high-level briefing issues to be considered before design work commences in earnest.
Project Outcomes	The desired outcomes for the project (for example, in the case of a hospital this might be a reduction in recovery times). The outcomes may include operational aspects and a mixture of subjective and objective criteria.
Project Performance	The performance of the project, determined using Feedback, including information about the performance of the project team and the performance of the building against the desired Project Outcomes.
Project Programme	The overall period for the briefing, design, construction and post-completion activities of a project.
Project Roles Table	A table that sets out the roles required on a project as well as defining the stages during which those roles are required and the parties responsible for carrying out the roles.

Project Strategies	The strategies developed in parallel with the Concept Design to support the design and, in certain instances, to respond to the Final Project Brief as it is concluded. These strategies typically include: • acoustic strategy • fire engineering strategy • Maintenance and Operational Strategy • Sustainability Strategy • building control strategy • Technology Strategy. These strategies are usually prepared in outline at Stage 2 and in detail at Stage 3, with the recommendations absorbed into the Stage 4 outputs and Information Exchanges. The strategies are not typically used for construction purposes because they may contain recommendations or information that contradict the drawn information. The intention is that they should be transferred into the various models or drawn information.
Quality Objectives	The objectives that set out the quality aspects of a project. The objectives may comprise both subjective and objective aspects, although subjective aspects may be subject to a design quality indicator (DQI) benchmark review during the Feedback period.
Research and Development	Project-specific Research and Development responding to the Initial Project Brief or in response to the Concept Design as it is developed.
Risk Assessment	The Risk Assessment considers the various design and other risks on a project and how each risk will be managed and the party responsible for managing each risk.
Schedule of Services	A list of specific services and tasks to be undertaken by a party involved in the project which is incorporated into their professional services contract.
Site Information	Specific Project Information in the form of specialist surveys or reports relating to the project- or site-specific context.
Strategic Brief	The brief prepared to enable the strategic definition of the project. Strategic considerations might include considering different sites, whether to extend, refurbish or build new and the key Project Outcomes as well as initial considerations for the Project Programme and assembling the project team.

Sustainability Aspirations	The client's aspirations for sustainability, which may include additional objectives, measures or specific levels of performance in relation to international standards, as well as details of specific demands in relation to operational or facilities management issues.
	The Sustainability Strategy will be prepared in response to the Sustainability Aspirations and will include specific additional items, such as an energy plan and ecology plan and the design life of the building, as appropriate.
Sustainability Checkpoints	The Sustainability Checkpoints ensure that key considerations in relation to sustainability are considered as the design and construction progresses.
Sustainability Strategy	The strategy for delivering the Sustainability Aspirations.
Technology Strategy	The strategy established at the outset of a project that sets out technologies, including Building Information Modelling (BIM) and any supporting processes, and the specific software packages that each member of the project team will use. Any interoperability issues can then be addressed before the design phases commence.
	This strategy also considers how information is to be communicated (by email, file transfer protocol (FTP) site or using a managed third party common data environment) as well as the file formats in which information will be provided. The Project Execution Plan records agreements made.
Work in Progress	Work in Progress is ongoing design work that is issued between designers to facilitate the iterative coordination of each designer's output. Work issued as Work in Progress is signed off by the internal design processes of each designer and is checked and coordinated by the lead designer.